No Nonsense Gardening Guide™

HERBS THE YEAR ROUND

By the Editors of Garden Way Publishing

Longmeadow Press

HERBS THE YEAR ROUND

Copyright © 1990 by Storey Communications, Inc.

Some of the material for this book has been adapted from *Growing and Using Herbs Successfully* by Betty E.M. Jacobs and from *The Pleasure of Herbs* by Phyllis Shaudys, both published by Garden Way Publishing. Used by permission.

No Nonsense Gardening Guide is a trademark controlled by Longmeadow Press.

ISBN: 0-681-40964-9

Printed in the United States of America

0 9 8 7 6 5 4 3 2 1

Prepared for Longmeadow Press by Storey Communications, Inc.

President: M. John Storey
Executive VP, Administration: Martha M. Storey
Publisher: Thomas Woll
Series Editor: Benjamin Watson

Cover and inside design by Leslie Morris Noyes
Edited by Kim Foster
Production by Carol Jessop, Joan Genova, Judy Eliason,
and Nancy Lamb
Illustrations by Charles Joslin

The name Garden Way Publishing is licensed to Storey Communications, Inc, by Garden Way, Inc.

Cover photograph © Walter Chandoha 1990

Contents

THE NO NONSENSE LIBRARY

NO NONSENSE GARDENING GUIDES

Flowering Houseplants
The Successful Vegetable Garden
Using Annuals & Perennials
Landscaping for Beauty
Herbs the Year Round
The Weekend Gardener

OTHER NO NONSENSE GUIDES

Car Guides
Career Guides
Cooking Guides
Financial Guides
Health Guides
Legal Guides
Parenting Guides
Photography Guides
Real Estate Guides
Study Guides
Success Guides
Wine Guides

CHAPTER 1

USING AND ENJOYING HERBS

Herb plants have served many purposes throughout history. In the days before showers and baths, strongly scented herbs were liberally strewn on the floors of homes and castles to improve air quality. Herbal lore includes methods of repelling insects and moths with combinations of strongly scented herbs. Long before the advent of modern medical science, people relied upon herbal teas and infusions for their curative powers. Herbs and spices were also used to disguise the flavor of spoiled food when there was no refrigeration.

In recent years, growing herbs has become one of the nation's most popular gardening endeavors — and for good reason. While flowers are grown for their beauty or scent, and fruits and vegetables for their fresh taste, herbs combine all of these features. Herbs that grace the landscape or the kitchen windowsill also provide a healthy dash of flavor to a wide variety of foods. And the sweet aromas possessed by many herbs can be used to fill a room with fragrance naturally.

Creative arrangements of herbs by color, height, and texture can make for a stunning landscape design. Many herbs serve as effective insect repellents in flower or vegetable gardens. And herbs grown indoors bring outdoor beauty and aroma to a home year-round.

Cooking with herbs offers a healthy escape from the heavily salted and artificially flavored foods offered in supermarkets today. Herbs can be dried or frozen to provide superb flavor, even through the winter months. Basil, oregano, tarragon, chives, dill, parsley, rosemary, thyme ... all will enliven a meal instantly, alone or in any number of combinations. Herbal teas, liqueurs, vinegars, sauces, soups, and breads are all sure to please, as are main dishes sprinkled with that special ingredient.

The fresh scents provided by herbs such as lavender, mint, lemon balm, and angelica make wonderful gifts when combined in potpourris, pomanders, wreaths, sachets, and bath oils.

What's more, herbs are easy to grow. They can be grown indoors at any time of the year, as well as outdoors. They are generally not as fussy about soil conditions as many other plants. The range of herbs available allows you to choose annuals, biennials, or perennials to suit your growing plan, and propagation can be carried out by seed, division, cuttings, bulbs, or simple layering. Most herbs can be grown in compact areas with minimum fuss and maximum enjoyment.

This book will introduce you to several of the most popular herbs — how to grow them and how to use them. And this is only a start. From here, you're bound to discover an endless variety of herbs and many splendid uses for them.

24 BASIC HERBS AND THEIR USES

Herb	Uses
Angelica	Attracting bees, cosmetics, flavoring, liqueurs, medicine, perfume, sugar extender, tea
Anise	Cosmetics, flavoring, insect repellent, liqueurs, medicine, perfume
Basil, sweet	Attracting bees, flavoring, insect repellent, medicine, perfume
Borage	Attracting bees, flavoring, medicine
Caraway	Cosmetics, flavoring, liqueurs, medicine
Catnip	Attracting bees, for cats, insect repellent, medicine, tea
Chervil	Flavoring, medicine
Chives	Flavoring
Comfrey	Compost-making, medicine, stock feed, as a vegetable
Coriander	Cosmetics, flavoring, liqueurs, medicine, perfume
Dill	Attracting bees, cosmetics, flavoring, medicine, perfume, tea
Fennel	Attracting bees, flavoring, liqueurs, medicine, perfume, tea
Garlic Chives	Flavoring, insect repellent
Lavender	Attracting bees, cosmetics, insect repellent, liqueurs, medicine, perfume
Lemon Balm	Attracting bees, flavoring, liqueurs, medicine, perfume, sugar extender, tea
Marjoram, sweet	Attracting bees, flavoring, medicine, perfume, tea
Mint	Flavoring, liqueurs, medicine, tea
Oregano	Attracting bees, flavoring, medicine, perfume
Parsley	Flavoring, insect repellent, medicine
Rosemary	Attracting bees, cosmetics, flavoring, insect repellent, medicine
Sage	Attracting bees, cosmetics, flavoring, insect repellent, medicine, tea
Savory	Attracting bees, flavoring, medicine
Tarragon, French	Cosmetics, flavoring, perfume
Thyme, garden	Attracting bees, cosmetics, flavoring, insect repellent, liqueurs, medicine, perfume, tea

Chapter 2

FIFTEEN BASIC HERBS TO GROW

Most herbs will grow well in a friable ("crumbly") soil that is enriched with lime and compost. They differ in hardiness and light requirements but, generally, they are all easy to grow. The exotic image of the herb shouldn't scare you off — you'll be surprised at how successful you will be.

There are hundreds of herb varieties that you can experiment with over time, but here is some basic growing information for fifteen of the most popular herbs to start out with.

ANGELICA (ANGELICA ARCHANGELICA)

Angelica blooms in its native Lapland on the eighth of May, the feast day of Michael the Archangel. Legend has it that the angel proclaimed angelica a cure for the plague.

Angelica is considered a biennial because it usually flowers, goes to seed, and dies in its second year. However, it sometimes takes up to three or four years to flower, making it the exception to the biennial rule.

Angelica prefers rich, moist soil in a partially shaded location. Be sure to plant it in the back of the garden, as it often reaches 5 or 6 feet in height

The plant is majestic, with large, light green, serrated-edged leaves and thick, hollow stalks. Early in the summer, angelica blossoms with huge clusters of white flowers.

Propagate by fresh, viable seed. Once a planting is established, angelica will reseed itself. Harvest the leaves and stems early in the season while they are still tender and colorful.

Angelica is an aromatic used to flavor liqueurs and wines. The candied stems decorate fancy pastries. Cook the tips and stalks with tart fruit to impart a natural sweetness.

ANGELICA

BASIL (OCIMUM BASILICUM)

In its native India, basil is a sacred plant, and its culture supposedly brings happiness to the household. In Italy, a gift bouquet of basil is a sign of romance.

Basil is a tender annual, very sensitive to frost. It is easily propagated by seed sown directly in the garden after the soil has warmed up. Basil likes a soil rich in organic matter and thrives on an extra dose of compost. Plant it in full sun and be sure to water it weekly in dry weather.

This fast-growing plant reaches about two feet in height and has large, egg-shaped leaves that curl inward. In midsummer, small spikes of white flowers shoot up from each stalk. Pinching off the blooms, or the tips of each stem before they flower, will make the plant bushy. The leaves can be harvested throughout the summer from the growing plant.

There is a "Dark Opal," or purple, variety of basil that beautifully offsets the greens and grays of the herb garden. It also imparts a rich magenta color to white vinegar.

Basil has a pungent flavor that superbly complements all types of tomato dishes. Pesto, a green sauce served on pasta, is made from ground basil leaves, garlic, olive oil, nuts, and cheese.

To dry basil, harvest the plant just before it blooms. Then hang the plant upside down, or screen-dry or freeze the leaves.

Chives (Allium schoenoprasum)

Chives are native to the East, and for centuries they were used to ward off evil and promote psychic powers.

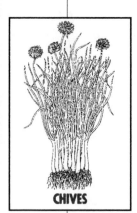

CHIVES

The plant is a hardy perennial, reaching 12 to 18 inches in height. The leaves — dark green, hollow spears — poke up through the soil in the early spring, almost before anything else. Mauve blue flower balls bloom on hard, green tendrils from midsummer on. These should be cut to keep the plant growing, but can be left on later in the season to keep foraging bees happy.

Chives prefer full sun, rich soil, and plentiful water. Mulching around the plants is helpful to keep competitive weeds and grasses at bay.

Propagate by seeds or root divisions. A small plant will quickly enlarge and should be divided every three or four years to keep the plant healthy. Simply cut through the plant with a shovel or sharp knife in the early spring, allowing at least ten small, white bulbous roots per new clump. Set the divisions 10 inches apart.

Harvest chives as soon as the spears are a few inches long. Snipping out entire spears encourages tender new growth. Chives do not dry well. Freeze them for winter use.

The delicate onion flavor of chives is used extensively in cooking. Chives can be added to omelettes, soups, cheeses, salads, or fish. The combination of sour cream and chives spices up many a baked potato.

DILL (ANETHUM GRAVEOLENS)

Dill has been used in the culinary arts for centuries, with the famed dill pickle being the most notable product.

Dill is a hardy annual that closely resembles fennel. However, it usually develops only one round, hollow main stem per root, and the feathery branches are a bluish green. Yellow flowers bloom in clusters of showy umbels. The dill seeds are dark brown, ridged, and strongly flavored. Dill grows 2 to 3 feet tall and can be planted in groupings to keep the plants supported in windy weather.

Propagate by seed sown directly in the garden. It does best in full sun in sandy or loamy, well-drained soil that has a slightly acid pH (5.8 to 6.5). Enrich your soil with compost or well-rotted manure for best dill growth. Once you have grown dill, it will reseed in following years.

Dill weed and dill seed are both used in cooking; the weed is mild and the seeds are pungent. Dill weed can be harvested at any time, but the volatile oils are highest just before flowering. It adds a delicate flavor to salads, fish, vegetable casseroles, and soups. The seed heads should be cut when the majority of seeds have formed, even

DILL

though some flowers may still be blooming. Whole dill heads look striking in jars of homemade pickles and flavored vinegar. Dill seeds add zest to breads, cheeses, and salad dressing. The seeds may be threshed from the heads after drying.

LAVENDER (LAVANDULA OFFICINALIS)

A hardy perennial, there are two basic types of lavender: tall-growing varieties and dwarf and semi-dwarf varieties. The tall-growing varieties grow about 30 inches high, requiring a light, well-drained soil and full sun. Liming the soil early in the season before planting is advisable. Propagation should be carried out using cuttings from 2 inches to 4 inches long, as soon as the new growth has reached that length, either in early summer or after harvesting, in early fall.

The dwarf and semi-dwarf varieties are the fastest growing

ones. There are a number of different varieties, including Mustead Dwarf, which grows about 18 inches high, and Hidcote Purple, which grows about 12 inches high.

The dwarf varieties produce their best perfume when grown in soil which is poor and gravelly; they also require full sun to thrive. Propagation can be by seed (though the plants are very slow to germinate, and very slow-growing) or by cuttings, taken as early in the year as they become available.

The best and quickest way to propagate lavender, though, is to divide three-year-old plants in the spring. They should be lifted and torn apart. Any piece with roots attached should be replanted deeply, so that all the woody stem is buried.

The oil distilled from the flowers of lavender is used in the perfume and cosmetic industries. It also has medicinal value.

LEMON BALM (*MELISSA OFFICINALIS*)

Lemon balm has softly hairy, oval leaves with scalloped edges and deeply veined surfaces. It is a hardy perennial that grows to 48 inches high.

LEMON BALM

Dry or wet soil, full sun, partial shade, or shade — lemon balm can take it all. Lemon balm spreads by seed and by runners produced after flowering. It is not invasive except in close quarters. To get lemon balm started, you can plant seeds in fall or early spring, make cuttings, or ask neighbors for volunteer seedlings or divisions of clumps from their gardens.

In early spring the leaves are a glowing green. In full sun lemon balm grows in a dense bush, sometimes quite close to the ground — about 6 inches tall. In shade, the plants may become up to 18 inches tall and grow more sparsely; they may reach 3 to 4 feet when in bloom. During summer, lemon balm leaves turn a duller green. The late summer flowers are white or pinkish and somehow manage to look like old seed heads even in full bloom. Plants die back to the ground in winter.

The leaves have a mild, slightly lemony flavor and a strong lemon candy scent. They do not taste sweet, but their scent can make them good additions to nonsweet foods such as tossed salads. They are most often used to flavor fruit juices, fruit salads, canned fruits, punches, wines, and herbal teas. You can also add them sparingly to meat, fish, and vegetables.

MARJORAM (*MARJORANA HORTENSIS* OR *ORIGANUM MAJORANA*)

Throughout history, marjoram has symbolized sweetness, happiness, and well-being. Shakespeare called it the "herb of grace."

Marjoram is a tender perennial native to the warm Mediterranean. In colder climates, it is grown as an annual. The plant reaches 8 to 12 inches in height and has short, branched, squarish stems. The small, oval leaves are grayish green and covered with a fuzzy down. Little balls or knots grow out of the leaf clusters and the end of the branches in midsummer. From these, white or pink flowers emerge.

Marjoram thrives in a light, rich soil in full sun. It prefers a neutral pH. Since it has a shallow root system, mulching around the plant helps to retain soil moisture and keep the weeds down.

Seeds can be sown directly in the garden after the soil has warmed up. Germination is slow, usually taking about two weeks. Keep the seedbed moist until the plants have sprouted. Marjoram can also be started from cuttings, layering, or division. Set transplants about a foot apart.

Marjoram is highly aromatic and its flavor improves with drying. Harvest just before the flowers open.

Marjoram is traditionally used in sausages and stuffings.

MARJORAM

MINT (*MENTHA* SPECIES)

Peppermint, spearmint, apple mint, and curly mint are but a few varieties of the fragrant mints used in gum, jelly, and liqueur.

Mints are hardy perennials and often reach 3 feet in height. They are notorious spreaders and will invade the surrounding garden territory if they are not confined. They prefer a moist, rich soil and will do well in full sun to partial shade.

Mint is known by its squarish stems and its tooth-edged leaves.   Clusters of white or purple flowers bloom off the terminal ends of the shoots.

Propagate by seed or division. Older mint plantings can be divided up every four or five years. Separate the roots into foot-sized clumps with a sharp shovel. These divisions make a nice present for a gardening friend.

The leaves may be harvested and enjoyed fresh throughout the summer. To dry mint, cut the stalks just above the first set of leaves, as soon as the flower buds appear. Hang to dry for 10 to 14 days.

Mint jelly is a favorite accompaniment to lamb roasts and chops, and minted peas are a special summertime treat.

OREGANO (*ORIGANUM VULGARE*)

Oregano's fame stems from the fabulous flavor it imparts to pizza and other Italian specialties.

OREGANO

Some confusion has arisen about the relationship between oregano and marjoram. They are, in fact, close relatives, and oregano is often called "wild marjoram."

Oregano is a hardy perennial that grows 18 to 30 inches tall. The oval, grayish green, hairy leaves grow out from the nodes. White or pink flowers make their showing in the fall.

The plant does best in a well-drained, sandy loam soil. If the pH is below 6.0, add lime before you set out the plants; oregano likes a sweet soil and a plentiful supply of calcium. Oregano thrives in full sun in a location sheltered from high winds. Mulch over the plant if winters are severe in your area.

Oregano may be propagated by seed, divisions, or cuttings. Because the seeds are slow to germinate, you will get the best garden results by setting out young plants spaced 15 inches apart.

To dry oregano, cut the stems an inch from the ground in the fall, just before the flowers open. Hang the plants upside down to dry.

PARSLEY (*PETROSELINUM CRISPUM*)

The Greeks believed that Hercules adorned himself with parsley, so it became the symbol of strength and vigor. Parsley was also associated with witchcraft and the underworld; it was never transplanted because this supposedly brought misfortune to the household.

Parsley is a hardy biennial, often grown as an annual. There are two main types of parsley: the Italian flat-leaved and the French curly.

During the first growing season, the plant develops many dark green leaves that are grouped in bunches at the ends of long stems. Italian parsley leaves are flat and fernlike; French parsley leaves are tightly curled. Umbels of yellow flowers are borne on long stalks. The plant reaches 12 to 18 inches in height.

Parsley thrives in rich soil that has been enriched with plentiful organic matter. It prefers full sun for optimum growth, but will survive in partial shade.

You can plant parsley from seed sown directly in the garden. However, since it takes three to four weeks to germinate, it is often more reliable to set out young plants. Space parsley transplants about 8 to 10 inches apart.

Pick fresh parsley throughout the season. To preserve parsley for winter use, cut the leaves in the fall and dry or freeze them.

Parsley is a popular kitchen herb, found with the fanciest steak or in the most common stew. It is a rich source of many vitamins and minerals, including vitamins A, B, and C; calcium; iron; and phosphorus.

ROSEMARY (ROSMARINUS OFFICINALIS)

Rosemary has been called the "herb of remembrance." This title may date back to the Greeks, who used it to strengthen the memory. It has appeared in religious ceremonies, particularly weddings and funerals, to symbolize remembrance and fidelity.

The perennial evergreen shrub grows 2 to 6 feet high, depending on the climate. It has woody stems, bearing thin, needlelike leaves that are shiny green on the upper surface and a powdery, muted green on the under surface. Blue flowers bloom on the tips of the branches in the spring.

Rosemary is a tender plant and must be sheltered or taken indoors for the winter in northern latitudes. It thrives best in a warm climate and prefers a well-drained, alkaline soil. Apply lime or wood ashes to acid soils testing below pH 6.5.

ROSEMARY

Start rosemary from cuttings or root divisions, because seed germination is slow and poor. This herb is a good candidate for container growing, allowing you to move it into protected quarters for the winter.

Harvest any time for fresh use. Hang up to dry for a winter supply.

Rosemary is a highly aromatic herb often used to flavor

13

meat dishes. Use only a few needles per pot, or the taste may be overpowering.

Sage (Salvia officinalis)

Although it is a prized culinary herb today, during past centuries sage was mainly cultivated as a medicinal herb. The name *Salvia* comes from the Latin, *salvere,* meaning 'to save', and it was believed that drinking a strong sage tea improved health and prolonged life. Needless to say, it was found in nearly every herb garden.

WINTER SAVORY

Sage is a hardy perennial, native to the Mediterranean. It grows 2 feet or so in height and has velvety, textured, patterned, grayish green leaves. The stems become woody as the plant matures and should be pruned out to keep the plant producing. Lavender flower spikes bloom in the fall.

Start sage from seed, cuttings, or divisions. Since the plant takes a long time to mature, transplants are usually set out. Space the plants 2 feet apart.

Sage prefers a well-drained soil in full sunlight. Enrich the soil with compost before planting, and add lime if the pH is below 5.8. Water well while the plants are young.

Harvest sparingly the first season and increase your quota yearly. The leaves can be picked at any time, but it is recommended that at least two crops a year, one in June and another in the fall, be harvested to keep the plants less woody. Hang stems up to dry in small bunches.

The flavor of sage is recognizable in stuffings. It especially complements heavy meats and game. Its flavor may overpower lighter herbs.

Savory (Satureia hortensis [summer], Satureia montana [winter])

Of the two savories grown for kitchen use, the summer variety is the mild annual and the winter is the sharper-flavored perennial.

Both savories have narrow, pointed, dark green leaves that grow out of the nodes. Small branches often arise just above the leaves. Lavender or pink flowers bloom in the late summer. Winter savory grows 8 to 10 inches tall; summer savory is slightly taller. Since they are small plants, the savories are good for container growing.

The savories prefer a somewhat dry soil and will survive even where the land is not too fertile. For the best flavor, plant them in full sun.

Summer savory grows well from seed sown directly in the garden in the early spring. Propagate winter savory by cuttings or divisions. Space both varieties 12 inches apart.

To harvest for winter use, cut the stems in the fall, just before the flowers bloom. Cut winter savory sparingly. Summer savory can be pulled out of the ground, since it will die anyway after one season. Hang up to dry.

These herbs are notably associated with bean dishes, ranging from soups to casseroles. Savory is also an essential ingredient in the *bouquet garni* seasoning mixture.

TARRAGON (*ARTEMISIA DRACUNCULUS*)

Tarragon enjoys a high standing in the kitchen, especially in French cuisine, where it lends itself to béarnaise sauce and *fines herbes* (a French herb blend).

Tarragon is a perennial plant, with the best varieties coming from the European countries. The Russian variety, on the other hand, is weedy and lacks essential oils. One way to distinguish between varieties is this: Russian tarragon produces viable seed; European varieties rarely do.

TARRAGON

Tarragon grows 2 to 3 feet tall and tends to sprawl out late in the season. The long, narrow leaves, borne on upright stalks, are a shiny, dark green. Greenish or gray flowers may bloom in the fall. Since it rarely sets seed, tarragon should be propagated by cuttings or divisions.

Tarragon prospers in infertile soil when provided with plentiful water and sunlight. It is advisable to mulch over the roots in the late fall to protect the plant from winter injury. Since tarragon becomes a rather large plant, it is often divided up every three or four years to make it easier to manage.

This herb may be harvested throughout the summer. To dry it for winter use, cut the stalks a few inches from the ground in the early fall. Hang them up or screen-dry them.

THYME (*THYMUS* SPECIES)

Native to the Mediterranean, this aromatic, perennial herb has many well-known varieties, including lemon thyme, creeping thyme, and garden (or common) thyme. Bees love it.

Thyme is a short plant, only about 8 to 10 inches tall. The leaves are small and narrowly oval, usually a dull grayish green. The stems become woody after a few years. Pink or violet flowers rise from the leaf axils in the early fall.

Thyme flourishes in sandy, dry soils in full sun. It is an excellent candidate for rock gardens.

Propagate thyme by seeds, divisions, or cuttings. The seeds, however, are slow to germinate, so it is best to set out transplants. Space thyme plants 15 inches apart. Older, woody plants can be rejuvenated by digging up the plant and dividing it in the early spring. Fertilize with compost or seaweed.

The leaves can be harvested for fresh use throughout the summer. To dry thyme, cut the stems just as the flowers start to open and hang up to dry in small bunches. Harvest sparingly the first year.

Thyme has many culinary uses and is one of the three essential herbs used in poultry stuffings, along with parsley and sage.

CHAPTER 3

GROWING HERBS INDOORS

One reason herbs have won favor among so many gardeners is that they are easily grown indoors as well as outdoors, so you can enjoy their fresh taste year-round. You can start your herbs from seed in the winter and transplant them to your outdoor herb patch when warmer weather arrives, or you can maintain a number of the smaller herbs indoors on your kitchen windowsill to harvest whenever you need them.

AN INDOOR HERB GARDEN

If you want to grow herbs but don't have the garden space, there's no need to despair. Herbs are some of the easiest plants to grow in containers. All they need is adequate light, warm temperatures, fertilizer, and humidity to thrive.

Choose herbs that you often use in cooking, or those that are hard to find in stores. It is preferable to select compact, low-growing herbs like **thyme, marjoram, savory, parsley, sage, basil,** or **chives.** You certainly would not want a 6-foot angelica plant on your windowsill! Help your herbs stay bushy and manageable by pinching off the terminal ends of their shoots.

Pots made out of porous materials are desirable to use for container gardening because they allow excess water to seep through. Most herbs cannot tolerate "wet feet." That's why clay pots are preferable to the plastic ones. Whatever type of container you choose, though, *a drainage hole is a must.*

Use a suitable growing mixture. A sterilized potting soil mix is your best bet. Bags of soil mixtures are available at most nurseries and garden centers.

Place a small piece of broken pottery or a few pebbles in the bottom of your container to keep the soil from spilling out of the drainage hole. Fill the container about halfway with soil mix. Then place the herb cutting or transplant in the pot and pack soil around it, leaving a 1-inch headspace. Water well.

Herbs are sun lovers. They should receive at least five to six hours of direct sunlight a day. Find the windows in your house where the sun shines most: south and east windows tend to receive the most light; west and north windows receive the least. You can also use fluorescent grow-lights if you lack sufficient natural lighting in your house. A combination of warm and cool white fluorescent tubes is recommended. Position the lights about 6 inches from the tops of the plants, and keep them on for 8 to 10 hours a day if they are providing the only light source for the plants.

SOME RECOMMENDED INDOOR HERBS AND THEIR CARE

PLANT	MAXIMUM HEIGHT	LIGHT REQUIREMENTS	SOIL
Basil, Sweet	18"	Full sun	Rich
Chives	8–12"	Full sun	Rich
Lavender, Dwarf	12–18"	Full sun	Well-drained, light
Marjoram, Sweet	9–12"	Full sun	Rich, light
Oregano	18"	Full sun	Light, dry
Sage	18"	Full sun	Sandy, limed
Savory, Summer	18"	Full sun	Light, rich
Savory, Winter	8"	Full sun	Poor, well-drained
Thyme	10–12"	Full sun	Sandy, well-drained

Herbs prefer day temperatures of 65° to 70°F. and night temperatures of about 55° to 60°F. Most houses tend to be dry in the wintertime; the more humidity you can put in the air, the better.

Let your plants dry out between waterings. Too much water has probably killed more container-grown herbs than too little. Feel the soil and make sure it is dry about an inch down.

Water the plants thoroughly so that the water flows out of the drainage hole. Finally, remember that plants are like people — they prefer a warm bath to a cold shower!

Potted herbs thrive on small, regular doses of water-soluble fertilizer. Treat them with a *dilute* solution of liquid seaweed or fish emulsion once a week. (Halve the recommended dosage.)

Although insects and diseases are rarely a problem with garden-grown herbs, you may occasionally encounter a pest on your indoor herbs. There are several common culprits, and they include:

Red spider mites. Cause a yellowish, mottled discoloration of the foliage. Can be seen with a hand lens. Wash the plant with a soapy water solution.

Whiteflies. Tiny, mothlike, white pests that suck the sap out of the leaves. They rise like a little cloud when the plant is disturbed. Wash with a soapy water solution. Pyrethrum insecticides also successfully combat whiteflies.

Damping-off. Characterized by wilting or rotting of the plant. This fungal disease is often a problem on overwatered herbs or newly started transplants. Be sure your potting mix is sterilized, and do not overwater. Thin plants to allow good air circulation.

Starting from Seed

Most herbs are easily propagated by seed, the most notable exceptions being varieties of comfrey, garlic, tall lavender plants, most mints, southernwood, French tarragon, and lemon thyme. For instructions on how to propagate these herbs, see Chapter 5.

Seeds of lemon balm, sweet marjoram, and parsley germinate best when soaked in water 24 hours before they are planted. To start seeds, fill separate pots or flats of soil mix for each herb to be sown. Tamp the soil down gently, leaving about ½ inch of space at the top. Shake the seeds out gently and sow them finely — not too close, or plants will be competing with one another for nutrients. Label each pot to record what you have planted; sow only one type of herb per container, to ensure that each variety is cared for properly. Cover the seeds lightly with soil: a depth of twice the size of the seed is good.

The best method of watering newly sown seed is to soak the pot in a shallow tub of water, allowing the soil to suck up water from the bottom. This ensures that the soil at the bottom receives water and prevents the seeds from floating, which may occur when you water from the top. The water level should rise only to about three-quarters of the height of the container. Be sure your tub or sink is large enough to allow for easy maneuvering of the pots, to prevent spillage.

Once the top surface of the soil is moist, lift the pot from the tub or sink and let it drain. Shade the pot with a sheet of glass covered by a layer of newspaper to limit the amount of light received. When any sign of sprouting appears, remove the glass but continue to let the newspaper shade the sprouts for a few days, then gradually expose them to the sun. It's best to continue watering from the bottom at this stage, keeping the soil moist but being careful not to overwater, either.

Bottom watering allows the soil to suck up the water it requires.

Some seeds, such as basil and sweet marjoram, need extra heat. Put a 15-watt light bulb inside a wooden box and place the containers on top of it to keep them warm.

Transplanting Seedlings into Pots

The next step is to plant your seedlings directly into individual pots. It's important to transplant into a proper soil environment to give the seedlings a healthy start. You can buy prepared soil mixes, or mix your own in the fall and allow it to cure over the winter for use the next spring. If you mix your own, be sure to mix the ingredients thoroughly to spread each of them evenly throughout the soil.

Transplant each seedling as soon as it grows its second set of leaves — called the "true" leaves — to be sure the root system is adequate. Choose a peat pot, a divided container, flats, or any of the other products available — 3 inches square for each seedling will be plenty of room. Then follow these steps:

1. Water the seedlings a few hours before transplanting, to help them resist the shock of being moved and to keep the soil moist enough so that it will cling to the roots during the move.

2. Using a small plastic knife, a small dibble, a doctor's tongue depressor, or the like, carefully lift the seedling from its original soil, trying to avoid any disturbance to the roots. Try to transplant some of the original soil along with the roots.

3. Dig a hole in the soil of the new transplanting pot and lower the seedling into it gently. Some of the stem should also be lowered into the hole. The soil should be warm and moist.

4. Plant seedlings an even distance from one another, and be sure they are standing straight. Press the soil around each firmly, leaving no air pockets. The soil should be packed evenly to create a level surface and to ensure that water will be distributed evenly.

5. Water from below once you've finished transplanting. Place

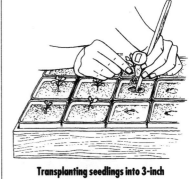

Transplanting seedlings into 3-inch square pots.

the seedlings in a slightly shady area at first, to allow the plants to recover from the shock. After the initial bottom watering, it will be safe to water from above. Add a liquid fertilizer every ten days to two weeks.

Choose only sturdy seedlings for transplanting — don't bother with weak or spindly plants.

TRANSPLANTING TO THE GARDEN

Before you set your transplants out in the garden you'll need to "harden them off" to prepare them for outdoor living.

■ Cut back on the amount of water and fertilizer you provide, beginning about ten days before you plan to transplant into the garden.

■ Set the plants outside for a few hours on a warm, sunny day. Place them in a sheltered location, so they will not be windblown.

■ Gradually increase the time you leave the plants outside on each succeeding day, until you finally leave them out all day and night.

It's best to transplant in cool weather, usually in the spring or early fall. Pick a day when the soil is not too moist and the sun is not shining.

21

Tip the pot upside down, holding on to the stem gently with your second and third fingers. Tap the bottom of the pot so the plant, along with the roots and soil, will fall into your hand in a clump.

Dig a hole in the soil slightly bigger than the root ball and fill it with water (or water and liquid fertilizer). Let the liquid drain into the soil, then place the plant in. This process is called "puddling" in the plants; it's done to water the roots, but not the topsoil — the topsoil should remain dry. Pack the soil around the stem, evenly, to create a level surface.

Water the plants at the first sign of drooping, and be sure to soak them thoroughly so that water reaches the roots.

A plant with roots and ball of soil attached will fall neatly into your hand.

"Puddling in" a plant.

CHAPTER 4

PLANNING AN HERB GARDEN

The herb garden need not occupy a large amount of space. A 4'x10' plot will provide plenty of room for 18 to 24 plants to grow. Check the site carefully to ensure that plants will receive optimum growing conditions, and consider plant color, texture, and height, choosing herbs that will enhance the attractiveness of your garden.

PLAN AHEAD

The best way to get your herb garden off to a good start is to plan it out on paper. Decide which herbs, what varieties, and how many of each you want to grow. If this is your first experience with herbs, start small and increase the size of your garden later. Here are some ideas to consider.

■ Locate the short, compact herbs in the front of your herb bed, the taller varieties behind them.

■ Give some thought to color combinations. You may want to arrange a green and gray garden, or brighten it up with purple basil and flowering annuals.

■ Decide if you want to grow only perennials in one bed, or if you want to mix in annuals and biennials.

■ Repeat herb varieties to create symmetrical patterns, or plant to create a "wild" look.

■ If you are fortunate enough to have an old stone walkway or a slightly sloping terrace, you can easily create a splendid herb rock garden. Space large and small rocks in a pleasing pattern. Then plant herbs so that they cascade over and between the rocks.

■ You can plant a traditional sixteenth-century knot garden, a beautifully sculptured arrangement. Plant three or four types of compact perennial herbs close together to make a low hedge "knot." Regular pruning is essential, and much maintenance is required for this formal garden. Some herbs that lend themselves well to a knot garden are dwarf sage, lemon thyme, dwarf lavender, and winter savory.

Another clever way to arrange your herb garden, or to incorporate herbs into a larger vegetable or flower garden, is to consider whether they make good neighbors. Certain herbs are natural bunkmates for other plants — one plant may ward off pests that harm the other, or perhaps both plants require similar soil conditions. Many herbs have proven quite useful in keeping garden pests away. Companion planting is a good way to keep plants healthy, naturally.

The following chart lists some herbs and their preferred companions.

COMPANION PLANTING WITH HERBS

HERB	INTERPLANTING IDEAS
Anise	Plant with coriander
Basil	Companion to tomatoes; dislikes rue
Borage	Plant in orchards or as a border for strawberries
Chamomile	Plant with cabbage and onions
Chervil	Plant with radishes
Chives	Companion to carrots
Coriander	Plant with anise; dislikes fennel
Dill	Companion to cabbage and its family; dislikes carrots
Fennel	Plant alone
Marjoram	Plant throughout the garden
Mint	Companion to cabbage and tomatoes
Oregano	Plant throughout the garden
Parsley	Plant with tomatoes
Rosemary	Plant with sage, beans, broccoli, cabbage, carrots
Sage	Plant with rosemary, carrots, cabbage; dislikes cucumbers
Savory	Plant with beans or onions
Tarragon	Plant throughout the garden
Thyme	Plant with cabbage

Certain herbs are also known to deter insects. If you're having trouble with a certain insect in the garden or in the home, consult the chart below.

INSECT CONTROL WITH HERBS

INSECT	HERB TO PLANT
Aphids	Chives, coriander, anise, lavender, pennyroyal, spearmint
Ants	Pennyroyal, peppermint, spearmint, tansy, southernwood
Bean beetles	Rosemary
Black flea beetles	Wormwood
Cabbage moths	Hyssop, rosemary, sage
Cabbage worm	Thyme
Carrot flies	Rosemary, sage
Clothes moths	Lavender, mint
Flea beetle	Mint, catnip, wormwood
Flies	Basil, tansy
Fruit tree moth	Southernwood
Mosquitoes	Pennyroyal
Plant lice	Pennyroyal
Tomato worm	Borage

ORNAMENTAL CHARACTERISTICS

Whether you want to create a separate herb garden or incorporate herbs into your flower or vegetable garden, here is a guide to some particularly attractive herbs, with suggestions for bringing out the full beauty of the herbs in your garden.

ANISE HYSSOP. Anise hyssop makes an excellent formal edging for a path, either alone or with a front row of shorter plants, such as parsley or dwarf marigolds. It can be grown in clumps near other plants with blue-purple, blue, or blue-green colors —

sage, lavender, and fennel are excellent complements.

BASIL. Basil looks good massed in beds and borders, edging paths, or growing in pots and window boxes. Dark Opal basil contrasts well with clear yellow flowers or with the bright, strong green of parsley; pink and lavender flowers make a close, harmonious combination. Little-leaf basil can be grown with fine-leaved plants like parsley or carrots and with small, bright flowers, such as dwarf phlox and signet marigold.

CHIVES. Combine chives with plants of similar textures — bunching onions, Chinese chives, ornamental allium, and sea thrift. Contrast them with thyme and curly parsley. They are best grown in a bed, where leaning leaves are less noticeable. They are most attractive in the spring, at which time they should be given a prominent place in the garden.

DILL. Although dill is small and blue-green when young, it will be most visible in the landscape when it is tall and covered with yellow flower umbels. A long-lasting, low planting, such as seed-grown sage, looks good in front of dill. Dill shows itself off to advantage near blue-green or gray-green leaves and blue flowers; blue salvia is an especially good companion. Dill flowers have a greenish tinge that looks sickly next to intensely yellow flowers or bright green foliage. Planting dill in thickly seeded beds eliminates the need for staking. Even if early flowering occurs, plants will still look attractive.

FENNEL. Fennel combines nicely with other feathery-leaved plants, such as cosmos, asparagus, and carrots; with the bold foliage of zucchini squash; with blue-green, gray-green, or bright green leaves; with yellow, orange, purple, blue, rose, or white flowers. It makes an excellent background plant or a bountiful hedge. You can grow it in rows, beds, or clumps of several plants together.

Copper fennel coordinates best with blue flowers and with medium green or brownish leaves. The subtle effect of its coloring can be lost near strong-colored plants.

LEMON BALM. Lemon balm plants look attractive growing in small clumps, in masses, or in rows as a bushy spring edging. At their best in early spring, they make an excellent backdrop for spring-flowering bulbs, viola, sweet William, forget-me-not, and spring food plants, such as red and light green lettuce and thyme and chives (with their spring flowers). Lemon balm also forms an attractive groundcover under spring-flowering trees.

Lemon balm, mint, and borage are a vigorous herb combination in partly shaded locations. All of them become more scruffy-looking as summer wears on and should be placed where summer-loving plants will grow up in front of them.

MINT. Mint is an excellent groundcover in the dappled shade of light-canopied trees and shrubs. Various kinds of mint can be used alone or combined with other sturdy groundcovers, preferably those that stay green in winter when mint dies back. Bugleweed is a good choice as a companion.

Mint can grow in containers. A pot of mint sunk into the ground near a water faucet will thrive and look pretty in the moist conditions. Corsican mint forms a low, mosslike mat that can grow over rocks, along a garden pool, or between the stones of a path.

Mint leaves, usually an intense green color, go well with other greens such as lemon balm, parsley, or celery, as well as with blue-green fennel, bunching onions, and savoy cabbage. The leaves are especially vivid early in the growing season, when they make an excellent background for the bright flowers of spring and early summer. Late in the summer mints look drab and belong in the background.

OREGANO/WILD MARJORAM. Oregano is an excellent groundcover, one that is especially useful on banks and eroded slopes, where its strong roots hold the soil well. Use it as a groundcover by itself or with creeping thyme; you might also use it as a lawn edging, since it can be mowed and will hold its own against grass. Plant oregano in clumps or large masses, or in rows as an edging plant. It can be combined with small spring flowers or with white, pink, blue, or purple flowers of late summer, such as heliotrope and verbena. Its texture and colors blend with a wide range of other plants.

PARSLEY. Parsley looks wonderful in borders, edgings, masses, planters, pots, and window boxes. It makes a fine combination with white, yellow, orange, red, blue, and purple flowers; pink and lavender are not as good. Bright green, dark green, yellow-green, and blue-green are all attractive foliage blends; gray-green doesn't work well. Fine-textured foliage plants, such as carrots and coriander, match parsley, and small plants with large leaves (romaine lettuce, for example) are good contrasts. Large, bold-textured plants are overwhelming.

Some effective combinations include curly parsley with lobelia, "Lulu" marigold, viola, or linaria; flat-leaved parsley with kale and gypsophila; and both kinds of parsley with small spring-flowering bulbs, such as dwarf narcissus and grape

27

hyacinth. As an edging plant, parsley can be used alone or combined with other bushy, long-lasting plants such as dwarf pepper and dwarf marigold.

ROSEMARY. In cold-winter climates, most rosemary plants available for landscape use (from nursery stock or homegrown seeds and cuttings) are small — 1 square foot or less. Older plants that are overwintered indoors may get leggy and need to be pruned back to a small size. Plan for small-scale use.

Erect rosemary is an excellent low edging, either alone or with dianthus, phacelia, dwarf phlox, or lobelia. It can also be backed by larger plants, such as sage and lavender. Plant rosemary in borders, beds, or rock gardens; it also makes a good pot or window box plant. Rosemary blends well with other plants of fine texture and subdued foliage color — gray-green or dull green — such as yarrow, summer savory, thyme, lamb's ears, and small-leaved succulents.

Prostrate rosemary works very well in window boxes and hanging baskets, in rock gardens, and along retaining walls, where it can trail downward. At nurseries it is sometimes possible to buy fairly large prostrate rosemary plants, 1 foot tall by 2 feet wide. In mild-winter climates, prostrate rosemary can be used as an evergreen groundcover, while erect rosemary can be massed in beds or lined up in hedges. It will grow taller and more impressive each year.

SAGE

SAGE. Sage is sturdy and versatile. You may want to plant more of it than you can eat, simply for the pleasure of growing such dependable plants in your garden. It forms a low, uniform hedge and looks good in mixed borders, alone or in masses. It is also attractive in pots and window boxes. Combine sage with either bold or fine-textured, small or fairly large plants, and use it as a companion for plants that have trouble standing up straight on their own.

Plant sage with gray-green plants such as rosemary, lavender, and eggplant, and with blue-green plants such as leek, bunching onions, and kale. Many of these foliage combinations are effective during summers, falls, and mild winters. Sage foliage provides a good backdrop for the blue and purple flowers of heliotrope, nierembergia, campanula, and lobelia, and the yellow and orange flowers of marigold, butterfly weed, and gold yarrow. The flowers of sage also combine well with the blue or purple flowers mentioned.

SUMMER SAVORY. Plant summer savory in small clumps, big masses, or dense, low hedges. Savory can also grow in containers in protected places. Its neat leaves blend well with other leaves that are not overwhelmingly large or bold-textured. Blooming summer savory is a great contrast to bright yellow flowers or to bright green foliage, such as that of celery, carrots, and parsley. You might also grow it along with colors similar to its own, such as those of "Dark Opal" basil and "Molten Fire" amaranthus. Pink or lavender flowers, such as aster, cosmos, alyssum, and scabiosa varieties, make good companions.

WINTER SAVORY. Winter savory is often used as a low edging plant and does well in containers. It also blends well with fine- or medium-textured plants. It is such a dark green that it looks somber growing alone in large masses, so plant it in small clumps with bright green plants nearby. The flowers go well with oregano flowers and other small, late-summer flowers of blue, pink, lavender, purple, white, or yellow.

THYME. Neat bushes of upright thyme can be lined up as edging plants, massed in beds and borders, or planted in pots and window boxes. You can combine them with other plants of similar texture, such as rosemary, lavender, and summer and winter savory, or of related colors, such as kale, lima beans, rue, and dusty miller. Dianthus, lobelia, pimpernel, linaria, and alyssum have fine-textured foliage and flowers that agree with thyme's lavender blooms. In spring, the foliage provides a good background for grape hyacinths and dwarf daffodils.

Creeping thyme makes a strong-growing groundcover along paths and lawn edges, up hills and banks, down retaining walls, and over the edges of pots, window boxes, and hanging baskets. You can plant it at the base of bushes, in rock gardens, in beds, in flower borders, and in planting strips between sidewalk and street. You might let it grow between flagstones in a path, although its growth will be slow if it gets stepped on often.

You can grow one creeping thyme variety alone, or combine different types if they are equally vigorous. Tall creeping thyme varieties and oregano thrive together in full sun.

Raised Beds

Permanent, raised-bed gardens are practical and attractive for herb growing. Raised beds stand 8 to 12 inches above ground level. They guarantee better drainage and warmer soil for the plants growing in them. There is a wide variety of materials you can use to contain the bed: bricks, cement blocks, stone, railroad ties, logs, or anything else that suits your fancy.

It is best to make the bed 4 feet wide if you can reach across it from both sides. Make it 3 feet wide if you have access from one side only. Make it as long or short as your space allows.

If you have a plentiful supply of fertile, loamy garden soil, use this to fill up the beds. If your soil is not the best, mix together:

- 1 part garden soil
- 1 part sand
- 1 part peat moss
- 1 part compost
- lime

and use this as your planting medium.

Plant on a raised-bed garden the same as you would on a ground-level garden.

SOIL PREPARATION

Herbs will prosper in most types of good garden soil, especially a fertile, well-drained, sandy loam. Since most herbs are native to the relatively poor, rocky soils of the Mediterranean area, they are able to make a fine showing under less than optimum conditions. However, if you are considering a long-term perennial bed, it is advisable to make your soil the best it can possibly be. Most soils benefit from the addition of organic matter, such as compost, chopped leaves, or peat

MAKING A RAISED BED

Making a raised bed with hand tools. Mark the bed with stakes and strings. Use a rake to pull soil from the planned walkway to the top of the bed. Stand in one walkway and pull soil toward you from the other walkway. Repeat the process on the other side.

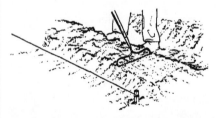

Level the top of the bed with the back of the rake. Sides should slope at a 45-degree angle. A lip around the top edge will help reduce erosion.

Making a raised bed with a tiller with a hilling attachment. Set the hilling wings to the highest position. Line up the center of the tiller in front of your first stake, point it at the stake at the far end of the bed, and guide the tiller directly toward it.

moss. Organic matter improves the texture of soil, making light or sandy soil more fertile and able to retain a greater amount of water, and loosening heavy or clayey soil.

Most herbs require well-drained soil (the exception being some types of mint). Well-drained means that water seeps down into the soil at a fairly constant rate, so there is never a pool of standing water on the soil surface that will result in soggy roots for the herbs. Do not plant in poorly drained areas unless you plan to build raised beds.

All soils should be tested before you start growing. The information you get from your soil test will give you a clearer understanding of your soil and its needs. You can buy a soil test kit and do your own testing or, for a minimal cost, you can send your soil off to a soil testing lab for analysis. Your county's Agricultural Extension Service can help you with this.

A soil test will determine the soil's pH (degree of acidity or alkalinity). A pH of 7.0 is neutral; below 7.0 is acidic, above is alkaline. Most herbs prefer a pH in the range of 6.0 to 7.5. If your soil is below 6.0, then it is too acid and you need to "sweeten" it with lime or wood ashes. Apply 5 pounds of lime to each 10 square feet of area to raise the pH one point. Add the lime the fall before planting to give it sufficient time to work into the soil.

A soil test will also tell you which nutrients are available in your soil and which, if any, are lacking. The major nutrients a plant needs for growth are nitrogen, phosphorus, and potassium. These are the main ingredients in most chemical fertilizers. However, all plants also need other essential elements for good growth. Some of these are calcium, magnesium, sulfur, and the many trace minerals. Most herbs require only small amounts of fertilizer and are sensitive to overfeeding.

The best time to fertilize herbs is in the early spring, just as they are planted or when they start to put out new growth. Organic fertilizers like compost, alfalfa meal, bonemeal, blood meal, or cottonseed meal will not damage the soil or poison your produce. Well-rotted or dehydrated manure can also be used. Fresh manure contains too much ammonia and may "burn" the plants. If the plants look as if they could use a lift later in the season — indicated by yellowing foliage and sparse growth — give them a shot of a liquid fertilizer, such as fish emulsion or seaweed, mixed with water.

You can use a complete chemical fertilizer, such as 5-10-10, if you desire. Just add a couple of tablespoons around each perennial shrub in the early spring. Then mix it into the soil and water well to send the nutrients down to the roots.

Most perennial herb gardens benefit from a layer of mulch. Mulch is material that is spread on the soil's surface to maintain even soil temperatures and moisture content. Mulch also discourages weed growth, primarily because it blocks out light, which prevents weed seeds from germinating. Mulching the herb garden cuts out a large percentage of the time you would ordinarily spend watering or weeding.

As an added bonus, organic mulches decompose and add fiber and nutrients to the soil. The following are several good mulches to use in your herb garden:

- Chopped straw, leaves, or hay (Do not use hay that has gone to seed.)

- Chopped bark

- Grass clippings

- Peat moss

Full-page photo: **Drying bunches of herbs in the kitchen.** JERRY HOWARD/POSITIVE IMAGES. **Inset: Broad-leaved sage (*Salvia officinalis*).** MADELAINE GRAY.

Full-page photo: Lemon thyme (*Thymus serpyllum*) used as a creeping groundcover. JOHN A. LYNCH: PHOTO/NATS. **Flowering sage (*Salvia x superba*).** ROBERT E. LYONS: PHOTO/NATS.

Full-page photo: Basil grown in containers with annual flowers and ornamental peppers. ANN REILLY: PHOTO/NATS. **Inset, top: Peppermint (*Mentha piperita*).** AL BUSSEWITZ: PHOTO/NATS. **Inset, above: Summer savory (*Satureia hortensis*).** MADELAINE GRAY.

Full-page photo: Harvested bunches of marjoram, chives, basil, sage, parsley, and rosemary. JERRY HOWARD/POSITIVE IMAGES. **Inset, below:** Sweet basil (*Ocimum basilicum*). MADELAINE GRAY. **Inset, bottom:** Oregano (*Origanum vulgare*). ANN REILLY: PHOTO/NATS. **Following page: Making an herbal wreath.** JERRY HOWARD/POSITIVE IMAGES.

CHAPTER 5

PROPAGATING HERBS

Most herbs can be propagated *vegetatively* — that is, by layering, division, or cuttings — instead of by seed. In fact, many herbs must be propagated vegetatively, as they do not seed: several varieties of lavender, comfrey, and mint, as well as French tarragon, lemon thyme, and southernwood *must* be propagated by one of the methods described below.

Vegetative propagation is often the method of choice for herb gardeners because it speeds up growing time and produces exact replicas of existing plants. In most cases, you're likely to have better results with vegetative propagation than with seeding herbs outdoors.

SIMPLE LAYERING

One of the simplest ways to propagate herbs is to copy one of nature's methods of propagation — layering. Decumbent branches that touch the soil sometimes sprout new plants. You can mimic this process by following the steps below. In simple layering, new plants remain attached to their parents during their development and have a ready source of nutriment until they are strong enough to survive on their own. It is a good method to use when propagating just a few plants, and it requires little supervision.

Layering can be done at any time of year, but it is advisable to layer in the spring to allow roots to grow in the early summer. Prepare the soil where the new plant is to grow if it is not already friable and well drained. Sand or peat moss applied the day before should do the trick. You might also want to add dried manure or compost.

Herbs that can be propagated by simple layering include marjoram, rosemary, sage, and winter savory.

DIRECTIONS FOR SIMPLE LAYERING

1. Choose a stem that bends easily, no more than ¼ inch thick for best results. Remove any leaves from the stem. Scrape bark from the underside of the stem — the part that will be buried in the soil. Scrape off a strip about twice as long as the diameter of the stem. Or, make a cut at an angle right before a leaf node, about halfway through the stem. Dust the wound with one of the many rooting mixtures on the market.

2. Scoop soil away from the spot where the "wounded" part of the stem is to go, making a depression of about 3 inches. The scraped part of the stem will be brought into the soil, and the tip will come back up to the surface.

3. Anchor the stem with wire. Wrap 8-inch pieces of the wire around the stem where it enters and leaves the soil.

4. Fill in the hole around the stem with soil, and pack it firmly. Water thoroughly.

SIMPLE LAYERING

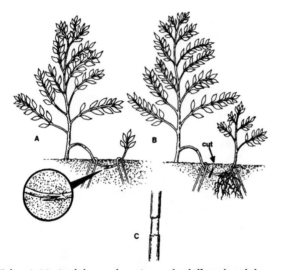

Make an incision just below a node, cutting at a slant halfway through the stem or branch. (A) Peg the branch down with 8-inch lengths of wire. (B) Six to eight weeks after layering, check for the root growth by moving soil away from the wound. (C) Scraping away the outer layer of bark is an alternative method to making an incision.

5. Place a brick or stone atop soil where the wounded part of the stem is buried to help keep it in place. This will also keep the soil below moist.

6. Keep the protruding tip of the stem erect. You can do this by setting up a small stake to keep the tip upright.

Six to eight weeks after layering, begin to check for roots sprouting from the buried wound by carefully digging the surrounding soil away. Roots form when organic materials en route to the tip of the plant's branches are diverted and accumulate at the wound. Replace the soil promptly, to avoid drying out the new roots.

Once a strong network of new roots has developed, separate the new plant from the old with hand pruners. First cut the branch just above the surface of the soil; then cut it back to the main stem, so that no dead stub remains on the old plant. Dig up the new plant and move it to its new location.

MOUND LAYERING

Bushy perennial herbs can often sprout several new herbs at once from just one plant. It's best to undertake mound layering in early fall so plants will be ready for spring.

Herbs that can be propagated by mound layering include garden, lemon, and bushy varieties of thyme, and winter savory.

DIRECTIONS FOR MOUND LAYERING

1. Mound soil up around the center of the herb plant, burying the central branches completely.

2. Be sure to keep these center branches covered with soil at all times. Replace the soil if wind or water washes it away.

3. In late spring, dig the plants up. Roots should have formed all over the buried branches, and any pieces with a few leaves and some roots can be cut off and replanted, either in pots or directly into the beds.

DIVISION

Another method of propagation is by division of the whole plant and its roots. This method is used for perennial herb plants that grow from a number of stems. It is not suitable for those that grow from one single central stem.

Division can be carried out in the spring as soon as growth is about to begin, and in early fall if plants are to be set out in the garden.

Herbs that can be propagated by divi-

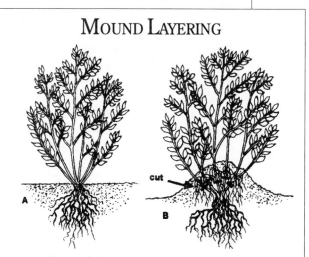

MOUND LAYERING

cut

A

B

(A) A suitable type of plant for stool or mound layering. (B) The same plant several months after it has been stool- or mound-layered, showing new growth on buried stems.

sion include bergamot, catnip, chives, English chamomile, garlic chives, horehound, hyssop, lavender (dwarf varieties), lemon balm, lovage, marjoram, oregano, pennyroyal, pyrethrum, sorrel, tansy, tarragon, thyme, winter savory, and woodruff.

Directions for Dividing Herb Plants

1. Lift the mother plant carefully with a fork.

2. Wash the roots with a hose gun to remove all the soil. The formation of the whole plant can then be seen, making it easy to see where to divide it.

3. Depending on the type of plant formation, either pull apart the plant or cut off the younger new plant growth around the central older growth. This old growth can be discarded. The new growth will supply you with new plants.

4. Trim some of the leaves and stems off the new little plants before replanting them. This avoids excessive loss of moisture while the plant is re-establishing itself. The roots should also be trimmed, to encourage new growth.

5. Small divisions can be potted into 3- or 4-inch-square pots.

Stem Cuttings

Most perennial herbs can be started from cuttings. Terminal cuttings are made from the soft wood at the tip of a branch (or stem). Heel cuttings are made from the base of the branch (or stem), where it joins the main branch (or stem) of the plant. There is also no reason why you shouldn't cut a center section for rooting, provided the growth of the plant is long enough to allow for this.

Cuttings may be taken whenever there is suitable material available. Usually by late spring or early summer the new growth is long enough. From 2 to 6 inches of this new growth can be used for each cutting, shorter cuttings making more compact plants than longer ones. Remove the leaves to check wilting, which is caused by transpiration.

Before taking your cuttings from the herb plants in your garden, have these items ready:

■ Pruning shears to cut material from stock plants

■ A piece of clean wood the size of a kitchen chopping board

■ An X-Acto or other utility knife with new, sharp blade

■ Hormone rooting powder — the mildest strength, marked "for softwood cuttings"

■ Large plastic bags and wet newspapers

■ Sterile material in which to root the cuttings. This may be clean, washed sand, perlite, powdered Styrofoam, vermiculite, or a mixture of sand and one of the others in equal proportions. Peat moss is *not* recommended, since it tends to get soggy. Whatever you use, do not pack it tightly around the stems. It isn't necessary, and makes it difficult to remove the rooted cutting without damaging it.

Directions for Taking Stem Cuttings

1. Fill flats or pots with rooting medium, and water it.

2. Cut material from stock plants in the garden with pruning shears or a utility knife.

3. Put this cut material between wet newspapers or in a plastic bag, making sure the bag is large enough, so as not to damage the stems or leaves.

4. Put a small amount of plant material on the cutting board and, using the utility knife, cut pieces of stem off just below a node. Some people insist that the cut must be at an angle, others that it should be at right angles to the stem. There seems to be little difference either way you cut. Try to keep the cuttings between

Insert the cutting about half its length into the rooting medium, at an angle of about 45 degrees.

2 and 6 inches in length. You may find you can make three cuttings from one stem: a tip, a center, and a heel cutting.

5. Strip at least half of the leaves off of each cutting.

6. Put each cutting in a plastic bag until you are ready to put it in the rooting medium. Do not prepare more than fifty cuttings before going on to the next step. (There is no reason that cuttings of different varieties of herbs cannot be put in the same flat or pot. Remember, though, to label them carefully with the name of the herb and the date when the cutting was taken. Use plastic or wooden labels, writing on them with a garden pencil or a *waterproof* felt pen.)

7. Dip the cut end of the cutting into the hormone rooting powder. (This step is optional — there is much controversy about the necessity of it.)

8. Gently tap off *surplus* rooting powder.

9. Insert the cuttings about half their length into the rooting medium, angled at about a 45-degree angle.

10. Repeat steps 7, 8, and 9 until the flat is filled with cuttings. Space the cuttings about 1 square inch apart.

11. Give the cuttings some shade for at least a week, then plenty of light, but no direct sunlight. Water them frequently.

12. To see if rooting has started, pull gently on a cutting. If you feel some resistance, the roots are forming. But if you are using sand alone as a rooting medium, do *not* pull. The sand holds so firmly, especially when wet, that there will always be resistance, whether the roots have formed or not. It will be necessary to lift a cutting out of the sand with a plant ladle or dibber, to check on root growth.

13. Transplant the cuttings into soil when the roots are about an inch long. There will be little, if any, new top growth at this stage.

14. Give the newly transplanted cuttings shade for a few days.

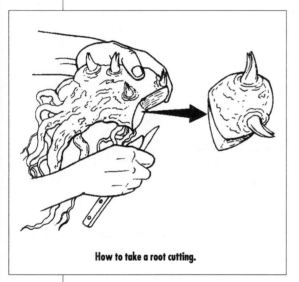

How to take a root cutting.

Root Cuttings

A few fleshy, thick-rooted herbs (for example, beebalm and comfrey) sprout several shoots from the tops of their roots. Propagate these herbs by slicing the root in pieces, so that each piece has some of the fleshy root and a bud. Then bury the pieces just below the surface of the soil, either in a pot or in the ground, and keep them well watered.

The best time to propagate by this method is in the spring, as soon as new growth begins, though with care it can be done at almost any time from early spring until fall, as long as the newly planted roots can be kept shaded and moist. If leaf growth has become heavy, remove most of it before replanting, leaving only a small center leaf, and plant so that the leaf remains above the soil and the piece of the root is below.

New, small roots will grow from the pieces of the old root, and, when the new leaf growth is well established, the new plant is ready to transplant to the garden.

RUNNERS

A runner is a trailing stem that will take root at its nodes. Sometimes the stem travels over the ground and sometimes under it. Herbs that propagate by runners include the various mints and pennyroyal. Propagating

PROPAGATION BY RUNNERS

Sever 2-inch pieces of root, with at least one node on each piece.

from either type of runner requires the same technique. It is best done in spring, when growth is just beginning, or after the final harvest in early fall.

DIRECTIONS FOR PROPAGATING BY RUNNERS

To prepare the material for planting as small pot plants:

1. Sever 2-inch pieces of root, with at least one node on each one.

2. Replant 1 inch below the soil, three pieces to each 4-inch-square pot.

3. Water.

To prepare material for planting in beds:

1. Sever 6-inch pieces of root, with several nodes on each.

2. Replant six to eight pieces per square foot of bed, depending on the amount of material available.

So there you have a rundown of the basic methods of herb propagation. Often, more than one method of propagation can be used successfully with a particular kind of herb, so you'll have a choice. Experiment with different methods for different herbs, and determine which is best for you.

Chapter 6
HARVESTING, DRYING, AND PRESERVING

A successful harvest is perhaps the most satisfying part of growing herbs. Dried or frozen herbs will add zest to your meals months after they've been picked, and harvest and preservation is relatively simple: herbs can be preserved by drying, freezing, or even in the microwave. So take some time to experiment and find your favorite method, and enjoy flavorful meals any time.

HARVESTING

Herb leaves, seeds, flowers, and roots can add flavor and color to almost any food. Except for the seeds, whichever part of the plant is used, it is most flavorful and best for drying when young and tender. Pick leaves and flowers when flower buds are about half opened; volatile oils are at their highest then. You can harvest in midsummer and again in the fall. If you are harvesting seeds, you should collect them when the seed heads are turning brown — too early means the seeds have not yet ripened, too late means the seed crop may fall to the ground and be lost.

Pick before noon, as soon as the sun has dried off the dew. If you live in a dusty area, or know heavy rains have splattered your herbs with mud, try hosing them off the day before you harvest them. By not washing them after they are cut, the herbs will dry faster, and you reduce the risk of losing some of the precious oils.

Don't try to "pick" herbs as you might daisies — breaking the stems leaves a ragged edge that is harder to heal, and pulling up on the stems may disturb the roots. Cut them instead. Pruning shears or scissors are fine for this. Leave 4 inches of stem on leafy annual herbs. Cut only one-third the growth of leafy perennials. In both cases this permits further growth — and further harvesting.

Creeping herbs such as thyme may need to be rinsed after harvesting. Hold muddy leaves under running water for a minute, shake, and pat dry with paper towels.

DRYING

The delicate flavors of herbs can be spoiled by heat and

faded by the sun. The flowers and green leaves of herbs should be dried at low temperatures and away from direct sunlight. Good air circulation is important in order to dry herbs quickly and thus preserve their flavor.

Dry leaves on their stems. It's easier to strip them off when dry than when green, and it's generally easier to dry them on the stem.

Herbs can be dried in a commercial dehydrator or in an ordinary oven. If a dehydrator or oven is used, herbs should be dried separately, in order to keep their distinct flavors from blending. This precaution is not necessary, of course, with outdoor drying.

Oven drying is a hotly debated topic: some people appreciate its speedy results; others denounce it because they say it vaporizes the volatile oils. If you want to give it a try, here's how it is done. Heat the oven to 150°F. Scatter the herbs on a baking sheet and put it in the oven, leaving the door ajar. Stir the herbs every few minutes. Remove the tray as soon as the herbs are crisp.

While the methods listed above are ideal for drying

USING THE MICROWAVE

The microwave oven has proven to be a useful tool for drying herbs. Place a single layer of herb leaves between paper towels. Then put the paper towels in the microwave and dry on high power for one to two minutes, depending on the thickness of the leaves. Cool and test the herbs for brittleness. Herb leaves are dry when they will crumble in the hands easily. If they're not dry, put them back in the microwave and allow them to dry one-half to one minute longer. You'll need to experiment a bit with this method to determine how long to microwave each herb, depending on type of herb and your microwave.

herbs, there's another simple method, one that's been used for centuries. Just pick and tie up small bunches of herbs, then hang them in a room out of the sunlight. They'll be dry in about two or three weeks and, in the meantime, will provide a decorative touch to the room.

An alternative to this method is to tie the bunch of herbs in a brown paper bag, with the stem ends tied at the mouth of the bag so the bunch hangs down inside. This reduces the light that reaches the herbs, prevents dust from settling on them, and keeps errant leaves from falling to the floor. The bags should hang in an airy room.

Screen drying works best with small quantities of herbs or

with leaves or seed heads that have been stripped off the stem. Spread a single layer of herbs evenly over a fine mesh screen and place it where air can circulate freely around the entire form. The herbs should be dry in a week or two. Once they are dry, store them immediately to reduce the loss of precious oils.

DIFFERENT METHODS OF DRYING HERBS

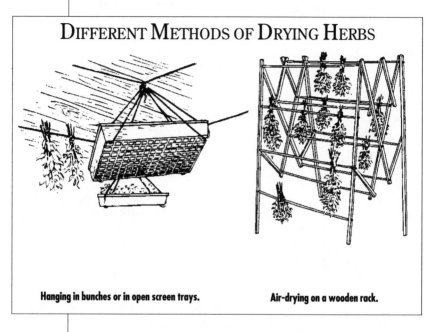

Hanging in bunches or in open screen trays.   **Air-drying on a wooden rack.**

FREEZING HERBS

Herbs can be frozen, too. In fact several herbs, such as chervil, chives, and fennel, lose their color and flavor when they are air-dried, and so are best preserved by freezing.

Freeze basil, burnet, chervil, chives, dill, fennel, parsley, and tarragon. It's best to blanch burnet, chervil, fennel, parsley, and tarragon in boiling water for one minute and then cool them in ice water before wrapping and freezing. The rest need only to be washed first. Remove leaves from their stems and wrap them in aluminum foil or plastic bags. (For the sake of convenience, wrap in packages you're likely to use at one time.) Place them in the freezer until you're ready to use them.

Another trick is to use ice cube trays to freeze small amounts of herbs. Add 2 cups of the herb to 1 cup of water and blend well in a blender. Pour this mixture into an ice cube tray and freeze. You can remove cubes from the tray and put them in plastic bags to make convenient serving-size packages.

STORAGE

Most herb leaves — with the exception of bay leaves — are cooled (if oven-dried), crumbled, and stored in glass jars. Some, such as sage, oregano, and marjoram, you can coarsely crumble in your hands. The leaves of rosemary, savory, tarragon, and thyme should be crushed fine with a rolling pin.

Store large batches of herbs in several small glass jars. Small containers will retain the flavors better than larger ones, which lose aroma each time the jar is opened. To keep dried herbs at their best, always keep the jars tightly covered in a dry, cool, dark place. If there is no dark storage area, jars may be kept in paper bags or in a covered can or box.

Do not store herbs in a cabinet near a stove, radiator, or refrigerator. The heat from any of them can cause a loss of flavor.

Use most dried herbs in their dry state, without refreshing them in water. The exception is rosemary, which should be added to the liquid of the dish and allowed to soak for a few minutes just before serving.

The flavor of dried herbs is much more pronounced than fresh herbs, so it is important to use very small amounts at first. To be safe, start with just a pinch. It is easy to add more, but the overpowering flavor caused by too much of a good thing can spoil a carefully planned dish.

HARVESTING AND PRESERVING TIPS

HERB	WHAT & WHEN TO HARVEST	HOW TO PRESERVE
ANGELICA	Side leafstalks in fall of 1st year; more often in 2nd year	Screen-dry leaves; freeze or crystallize stalks
ANISE	Flowers & leaves when seeds turn brown	Screen-dry leaves & seeds
ARTEMISIA (Silver)	Flowering stems when seed-heads are whitest in late summer	Dry in bunches, vases, or wreath shape
BASIL	Prune top ½ of plants whenever lush growth before flowering	Screen-dry, then oven-crisp. Or oil, vinegar, freezer or pesto
BAY, SWEET	Individual leaves sparingly until established; then top ¼ when lush or when transplanting to larger pots	Screen-dry
BERGAMOT	Top ½ of plant when flowering	Dry in vases, bags or bunches

43

BORAGE	Prune tops for early leaf harvest; then top ½ when flowering	Screen-dry leaves; candy flowers
CALENDULA	When flowering	Screen-dry
CARAWAY	Seedheads when brown	Screen-dry
CATNIP	Top ½ early and late summer before blossoming	Bunches or bags
CHAMOMILE (Annual)	Top ½ when flowers turn from gold to brown; leave some to self-sow	Screen-dry, or bags
CHAMOMILE (Perennial)	Prune as desired if for ground-cover	Screen-dry
CHERVIL	Outer leaves in fall and 2nd spring; preserve central growth and some seedheads	In butter, oil, or freezer
CHIVES	Snip outer leaves regularly all season; cut flowers in spring	Scissor-snip for freezer; vinegar
COMFREY	Top ½, or more, 2 or 3 times during lush summer growth	Screen-dry
CORIANDER	Foliage as needed, but allow some to go to seed; harvest when seeds turn brown	Seedheads in bags; leaves in oil or freezer
DILL	Top ½ of plants when seed-heads are beige; may trim foliage lightly earlier	Bunches or oil; vinegar or freezer
FENNEL	Whole plant when flowering; may trim foliage earlier	Screen-dry or vinegar, oil or freezer
FENUGREEK	Seedpods when ripe in fall	Screen-dry or syrup
GERANIUMS, SCENTED	Prune whenever lush growth	Screen-dry or candy or jelly
HOREHOUND	Top ½ when flowering, but may prune leaves in spring & early fall	Bunch dry; candy
HYSSOP	Top ⅓ in early & late summer	Bunch dry
LAVENDER	Cut back top ⅓ of branches just before flowers open up	Screen, bunch, vase
LEMON BALM	Top ½ early, mid, or late summer, before flowering	Bunch or bag; candy, vinegar or jelly
LEMON VERBENA	Top ½ midsummer & early fall before bringing inside	Screen-dry, candy or jelly

MARJORAM	Top ⅓ midsummer & early fall before flowering	Screen-dry, then oven-crisp
MINTS	Top ½ or more, in late spring, midsummer, & early fall	Bunch or bag-dry. Candy, ice cubes, vinegar, jelly
OREGANO	Cut top ½ in summer before flowering and in early fall	Bunch or bag-dry, then oven-crisp; vinegar, oil'
PARSLEY	Outer leaves when lush, leaving central growth	Bunch, oven, or freeze-dry
PENNYROYAL	Prune in early summer; top ½ when flowering in fall	Screen-dry
PINEAPPLE SAGE	Top ⅓ when lush foliage	Screen-dry or bunches
ROSEMARY	Top ¼ when established & lush in northern gardens or pots	Screen-dry, bunches, oil or vinegar or jelly
SAGE	Prune top ⅓ in early spring & again in midsummer	Screen-dry or bunches; oil, vinegar or freezer
SOUTHERNWOOD	Cut back by ⅓ in early spring; ½ of plant in late summer	Bunches or in open paper bags
SUMMER SAVORY	Top ½ in midsummer & early fall before flowering	Screen-dry
TANSY	Can prune in mid-spring & then cut top ½ or more when flowering in fall	Bunch or vase-dry
TARRAGON (French)	Prune top ½ in mid-spring, summer, & fall	Vinegar, oil, or freezer, cubes, or screen-dry
THYME	Top ⅓ in spring when lush & before flowering in summer	Screen-dry or vinegar, oil, or jelly
WINTER SAVORY	Prune tops lightly when lush growth in spring & summer	Screen-dry
WORMWOOD	Cut back top ½ in late spring, late summer, & mid-fall	Bunch or vase-dry

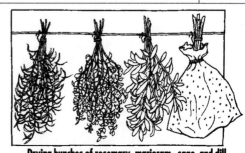

Drying bunches of rosemary, marjoram, sage, and dill.

Chapter 7

Cooking with Herbs

It is said that the sense of smell has the longest memory of all the senses. Doesn't the aroma of cookies baking recall memories of childhood? Doesn't the scent of the salt air stir your thoughts to crashing surf, long walks on hot sand, idyllic summers at the ocean? Herbs will create culinary memories as you incorporate them into your store of favorite ingredients. Cooking with herbs is a double pleasure. Not only do we please our palates, but we also delight our olfactory senses with the wonderful fragrance of the kitchen.

Herbs and spices have been used for centuries to enliven the taste of food, though both should be used sparingly. *Herbs* are the leaves and seeds of succulent plants grown in temperate climates. *Spices* are the seeds, bark, roots, pods, and flowers of plants grown in the tropics. Cayenne pepper, the one exception, grows all over the world. Spices offer a wide range of seasonings, from the subtle flavor of a dash of nutmeg in a custard to the hot, spicy taste of an Indian curry. Herbs, on the other hand, offer a subtle, gentler way to season foods.

Herbs will not assault your taste buds or cause your eyes to water or your throat to burn; instead, they provide a gentle enrichment to the natural taste of food. Think how much more refreshing a glass of iced tea becomes with a sprig of mint added. And, while the flavors of herbs are all subtle, their variety is great.

Some herbs are destined to blend with certain foods. Imagine a sliced, fresh tomato that has been warmed on the vine by the sun, drizzled with olive oil, and topped with fresh basil leaves. Cucumbers take on elegance when combined with dill and sour cream or yogurt.

Many culinary herbs have been used throughout history— in soups, stews, flavored butters, vinegars, dips, salads, meats, and vegetable dishes. Some herbs are even used in sweets, though herbs are more often associated with savory dishes. Due to climate and availability, different cultures rely on different herbs and spices in their cuisines. For example, the Scandinavians use dill in many dishes, and ginger is used extensively in Oriental cooking. The Mexicans use cumin, chilies, and oregano, while the Southern Europeans rely on basil, garlic, and oregano. American cuisine is such a melting pot of foods from around the world that the cook can select from a vast array of seasonings without being limited by tradition or availability.

Here are some guidelines to help you get started on the herbal adventure. They indicate some appealing blends between certain foods and ten popular herbs.

Ten Popular Culinary Herbs

There are hundreds of varieties of herbs for many different purposes. For culinary uses, the ten described here should definitely be included in your garden. These herbs appear in many recipes, and they blend well with a wide variety of foods.

Using the guidelines here and in the chart on page 49, you can begin substituting herbs for salt in favorite recipes and on new foods. Eggs without salt are not necessarily bland; with some tarragon, chives, or dill, they become savory and delicious. The taste for salt is learned or acquired and can, therefore, be *un*learned.

Use herbs sparingly — you can always add more if you wish. Add herbs in the last 20 to 30 minutes of cooking. They tend to lose flavor with prolonged cooking.

Basil

Basil is a highly fragrant, versatile herb that goes well with many foods. It is one of the best herbs to add to tomatoes, eggs, mushrooms, and pasta. What would spaghetti sauce be without it? Italians love it so much they mash large quantities of the fresh leaves with garlic, olive oil, cheese, and nuts to make their delicious pesto sauce.

Chives

Chives offer a mild onion flavor that doesn't hold up well when cooked. Chopped chives in sour cream on a baked potato is delicious. Chives combine well with cheeses and eggs. They are delicious in cold soups and sauces. Because of their delicate flavor, chives should be added at the last minute.

Dill

Dill is versatile. Both its leaves, known as dill weed, and its seeds are used in cooking. The combination of dill, cucumbers, and vinegar is well known and loved as pickles or cucumber salad. Dill complements the delicate flavor of fish, especially

47

salmon. It is a major ingredient of the traditional Swedish dish, gravlax, which is essentially salmon marinated in dill weed. Dill also adds zest to breads, cheeses, yogurt, and sour cream. It blends well with mustards and vinegars, providing a strong, refreshing flavor.

MARJORAM

Marjoram's sweet and spicy taste and delightful fragrance is provided by the fresh, dried, or ground leaves. An excellent herb to blend with meats, marjoram blended with butter is also delicious on hot vegetables. It is especially good with summer squash and wonderful with potatoes.

MINT

Many species of mint are used to flavor summertime beverages, teas, jellies, candies, and many other foods. A sprig of fresh mint in a glass of iced tea or lemonade turns the mundane into the special. Mint adds a refreshing zip to peas, new potatoes, and tender young carrots and parsnips. Lamb without mint sauce or mint jelly seems incomplete.

OREGANO

Oregano is native to the Mediterranean region, where it is used extensively in cooking. Its pungent flavor is used in herbal blends to shake on food instead of salt. It is an important ingredient in many Mexican and Italian recipes. Oregano goes well with most meats and vegetables, and works especially well with tomatoes, sauces for pasta, and pasta salads. In Italian tomato sauce and on pizza, oregano is a must.

PARSLEY

Also native to the Mediterranean, this mild-flavored herb is an excellent source of vitamins A and C. Parsley is used ubiquitously as a garnish, but it is also a refreshing, flavorful ingredient for soups, meat dishes, cheese and egg dishes, and herbal butters. Because of its mild taste, it can be used generously. Parsley softens the flavor of garlic.

ROSEMARY

Rosemary was used as a strewing plant in Mediterranean countries because its strong, sweet fragrance was thought of as a disinfectant. It blends well with all meats and, though associ-

Full-page photo: Opal basil and ornamental peppers. ANN REILLY: PHOTO/NATS. Inset: Chamomile (*Chamaemelum nobile*) used as a spreading groundcover plant. ANN REILLY: PHOTO/NATS.

Full-page photo: Lavender (*Lavandula officinalis*) used as a landscape plant. JERRY HOWARD/POSITIVE IMAGES. Inset, below: Anise hyssop (*Agastache foeniculum*). ANN REILLY: PHOTO/NATS. Inset, bottom: Lemon balm (*Melissa officinalis*). ROBERT E. LYONS: PHOTO/NATS.

Full-page photo: Dill (*Anethum graveolens*). JERRY HOWARD/POSITIVE IMAGES. **Inset, below: Rosemary (*Rosmarinus officinalis*).** ROBERT E. LYONS: PHOTO/NATS. **Inset, opposite page: Making tarragon vinegar.** JERRY HOWARD/POSITIVE IMAGES.

Full-page photo: Chives (*Allium schoenoprasum*). JERRY HOWARD/POSITIVE IMAGES. **Inset: Growing chives and parsley in containers.** PRISCILLA CONNELL: PHOTO/NATS.

Full-page photo: Caraway (*Carum carvi*). ANN REILLY: PHOTO/NATS. **Inset, left: Red yarrow (*Achillea millefolium* 'Kelwayi').** MADELAINE GRAY. **Inset, right: Tansy (*Tanacetum vulgare*).** DAVID M. STONE: PHOTO/NATS.

ated particularly with lamb, it goes equally well with poultry and pork. The aroma that fills the kitchen when sprigs of rosemary are laid on pork roasts or chicken breasts cooking in the oven is unbelievably delicious.

Tarragon

Tarragon's slightly licorice or anise flavor is subtle and complex, though it tends to dominate other herbs. Tarragon is a favorite of the French, who use it frequently in oil and vinegar dressings (vinaigrette) for lettuce. It also goes well with chicken, with eggs in omelettes, with fish, and in herbal butters. Adding tarragon to white wine vinegar is a widely accepted practice borrowed from the French. Perhaps because of its French connection, tarragon is associated with sophisticated, elegant cooking.

Thyme

Thyme is pungent and sweetly fragrant; it is also strong, and should be added to recipes with care. Thyme is as good dried as fresh. It is widely used in vegetable juices, soups, meats, and vegetables. A little thyme sprinkled on peas while they are cooking adds a savory touch. Thyme is a traditional ingredient of New England clam chowder. A little of this wonderfully tasty herb goes a long way.

Cooking Guidelines for Ten Popular Herbs

HERB	RECOMMENDED FOODS	FOOD	RECOMMENDED HERBS
Basil	Tomatoes, tomato sauces, pasta, eggs, meats (especially lamb)	Eggs	Basil, chives, dill, tarragon, oregano — many herbs blend well with eggs
Chives	Cold soups, salads, dips. Loses flavor in cooking	Cheeses	Basil, dill, marjoram, mint, parsley, tarragon
Dill	Cucumbers, fish (especially salmon), potatoes, sour cream, yogurt, eggs	Meats and Poultry	Tarragon, rosemary, marjoram, thyme

Marjoram	Beef, chicken, vegetables	Beef Pork	Oregano, marjoram Thyme, rosemary
Mint	Beverages, cold soups (especially fruit soups), lamb, teas, fruits	Lamb Fish	Mint, basil Dill, tarragon, thyme
Oregano	Tomatoes, tomato sauces, pasta, eggs, ground beef, Mexican and Italian dishes	Vegetables and Tomatoes	Basil, oregano, parsley
Parsley	Garnishes, salads — goes with most everything	Green vegetables Carrots	Thyme, marjoram, oregano Dill, mint
Rosemary	All meats (especially pork roasts and poultry), carrots	Winter squash Summer squash	Rosemary Thyme, oregano
Tarragon	Eggs, chicken, fish, salad dressings, vinegar, sauces	Potatoes Cabbage	Dill, chives Parsley, marjoram, dill seeds
Thyme	Vegetables, soups and stocks, clam chowder, chicken, meat sauces, poultry stuffing	Fruits	Mint

HERB MIXTURES

The flavors of some dried herbs are so compatible when used together, that they have become traditional companions in certain dishes. The following are some of the favorite herb blends.

BOUQUET GARNI

2 sprigs, or 6 tablespoons, dried parsley
3 tablespoons dried celery leaves
3 tablespoons dried onion, chopped
1 sprig, or 3 tablespoons, dried thyme

Tie all herbs in a small piece of cheesecloth and immerse in a pot of simmering soup or stew. Remove and discard before serving.

Chili Powder

1   tablespoon dried mild chili peppers, chopped
¼   teaspoon dried hot chili peppers, chopped
1   teaspoon dried cumin seed
1   teaspoon dried oregano leaves
½   teaspoon dried garlic
1   teaspoon salt

Combine all herbs and pulverize to a coarse powder with a mortar and pestle or in a blender. Use in chili, barbecue sauce, bean dishes, or meat loaf.

Fines Herbes

Fines herbes is a French term for a combination of herbs used for specific dishes. They are finely chopped, mixed, and added to dishes just before serving. The following are some *fines herbes* combinations.

For Pork Dishes

1   teaspoon dried sage
1   teaspoon dried basil
1   teaspoon dried savory

For Beef Dishes

1   teaspoon dried rosemary
1   teaspoon dried parsley
¼   teaspoon dried garlic

For Poultry Dishes

1   teaspoon dried sage
1   teaspoon dried savory
1   teaspoon dried parsley

For Lamb Dishes

1   teaspoon dried parsley
1   teaspoon dried rosemary
1   teaspoon dried marjoram

CHERVIL

For Fish Dishes

1   teaspoon dried chervil
1   teaspoon dried parsley
1   teaspoon dried savory

51

For Bean Dishes

1   teaspoon dried savory
1   teaspoon dried onion
1   teaspoon dried parsley

Poultry Seasoning

1   teaspoon dried sage
1   tablespoon dried thyme
1   tablespoon dried marjoram
1   tablespoon dried savory
1   tablespoon dried rosemary

Add 1 or 2 teaspoons of this mixture to any stuffing recipe.

Dips

Herb Dip

This flavorful dip is perfect for a platter of fresh vegetables cut into bite-size pieces (crudités). It could be made entirely with cottage cheese, or, for a more tangy flavor, yogurt could be substituted for the sour cream.

1   cup cottage cheese
½   cup sour cream
2   tablespoons minced onion
2   tablespoons wheat germ
2   teaspoons fresh thyme (or ¼ teaspoon dried thyme)
2   tablespoons chopped fresh parsley
4   drops Tabasco sauce
¼   teaspoon oregano
    Freshly ground pepper to taste

Mix all the ingredients in a bowl. Then transfer to a small serving bowl, garnish with fresh parsley or thyme, and surround with crisp fresh vegetables, such as cucumber spears, carrot circles, broccoli flowers, and mushroom slices.

Makes 1½ cups.

Herbed Party Cheese

This is so much better than the herb-and-garlic and black pepper cheeses you can buy that you'll never go back to them again. You can adjust the amount of garlic up or down to suit your taste (this recipe calls for a medium amount) or multiply the ingredients to make larger batches. The small amount of vinegar adds a lot to the taste.

6 ounces cream cheese or Neufchatel
½ teaspoon pressed or finely minced garlic
1 teaspoon Tarragon Vinegar (see recipe page 55)
½ teaspoon freshly ground black pepper
4 teaspoons milk
2 tablespoons mixed aromatic fresh herbs (or 2 teaspoons dry herbs plus 4 teaspoons parsley)
Salt to taste (optional)

Combine all the ingredients in a small bowl, mixing well. Serve with freshly made toast squares, Melba toast, or crackers.

Makes about ¾ cup.

Note: You can use the cheese right away, but it will be even more delicious after being aged for a day or two, covered, in your refrigerator.

Guacamole

This Mexican sauce of mashed avocados may be served as a dip with tortilla chips or used as a topping on Mexican dishes. The lime juice keeps the avocado from darkening, but if not served within an hour, it will begin to darken anyway. Placing plastic wrap directly on top of the sauce will slow down the darkening process. For a slightly different taste, lemons may be substituted for the limes.

2 medium-ripe avocados (soft to the touch)
½ cup chopped and seeded tomato
¼ cup fresh lime juice (juice of 2 limes)
1 tablespoon minced onion
¼ teaspoon Tabasco sauce
1 tablespoon chopped cilantro(or 1 teaspoon dried)
¼ teaspoon ground cumin
Freshly ground pepper to taste

Cut the avocados in half and remove the pits. Scoop the flesh out with a spoon and mash it with the back of a fork. Add the remaining ingredients and mix well. The guacamole should be lumpy.

Makes 1½ cups.

Herbal Tea Blends

For variety and a delicious blending of flavors, try combinations of dried herb leaves to make your own herbal teas.

Herb-Blend Tea

2   tablespoons dried rose hip slices
3   tablespoons dried peppermint leaves, crumbled
2   tablespoons dried orange blossoms, crumbled

Simmer dried rose hips in 1½ quarts water for 15 minutes. Remove from the heat. Add peppermint leaves and dried orange blossoms and let steep 5 minutes.

Solar Iced Tea

Most herbal teas can be made in this energy- and vitamin-saving way. Just place ½ cup dried herbs in a 2-quart clear glass jar. Fill with cold water to within 1 inch of the top. Screw the lid on tightly and shake well. Place in the sun for 5 to 6 hours. Strain off the liquid and add sugar or honey. Chill before serving.

Herb Butters

Add 1 teaspoon dried dill, chives, chervil, fennel, marjoram, or tarragon to ½ cup butter or margarine. Blend well. Cover and leave at room temperature for 2 hours to blend flavors.

Herb butter may be stored for several days in the refrigerator. To use, spread over fried or broiled meat or fish. You can also add herb butter to scrambled eggs just before serving or spread it on bread when making sandwiches.

"HERBALIZING" STORE-BOUGHT TEAS

Add interest and flavor to any commercial tea blend by adding ¼ teaspoon dried peppermint, spearmint, lemon balm, or thyme to a pot of steeping tea.

Oils and Vinegars

Herbal oils and vinegars make great gifts, and wonderfully complement your recipes. The following oil and vinegar recipes can be used as ingredients in some of your main dish recipes.

Garlic Oil

Using garlic oil in recipes provides a simple way to add the flavor of garlic without going through a lot of peeling, mincing, or pressing every time.

1   cup olive or salad oil

2 tablespoons garlic, peeled and finely minced

Combine the oil and garlic in a screw-top jar. Put the lid on tight. Let sit for 2 weeks before using.

Garlic-Ginger Oil

With this oil on hand, you're well on the way to a stir-fry whenever the mood strikes. Try it in non-Oriental dishes, too. Ginger and garlic go well with most vegetables, meats, poultry, or fish.

1 cup olive or salad oil
1½ tablespoons minced garlic
1½ tablespoons minced fresh ginger

Combine all the ingredients in a screw-top jar. Seal the jar and store, refrigerated, for 2 to 3 weeks before using.

To use, either stir or shake well if you want to use some of the garlic and ginger along with the oil. If not, just pour or spoon off the flavored oil from the top of the jar.

Basil and Other Single-Herb Vinegars

Consider this recipe as a pattern to follow — you can substitute any other fresh herb for the basil. Dill, for instance, makes a great vinegar, as does chervil. Tarragon creates a classic cooking and

Fill a dry, sterilized jar with washed, dried herbs. Store the jar in a cool, dark place for 4-6 weeks.

salad vinegar. Chives make a subtle vinegar — be sure to use a lot of them in the bottles. For small-leaved herbs such as thyme, use an extra sprig or two.

4 large sprigs fresh basil
2 cups white wine or champagne vinegar

Put the basil sprigs into a pint bottle and pour in the vinegar (or divide everything between two smaller bottles).

Seal. Store for 4 to 6 weeks before using.

Rosemary-Tarragon Vinegar and Other Combination Vinegars

Rosemary and tarragon are a terrific flavor combination, and the sprigs of the two herbs look attractive and exotic together in the bottle.

There are plenty of other good combinations, too; almost any herb goes well with any other herb. You can also use several herbs in combination. Oregano and dill are interesting together, as are basil and savory.

2 large sprigs rosemary
2 large sprigs tarragon
2 cups white wine or champagne vinegar

Make this just as you would the basil vinegar above. If you're dividing it between two bottles, make sure to put a sprig of rosemary and a sprig of tarragon in each.

APPETIZERS AND SOUPS

PEASANT CAVIAR

This is also known as Eggplant Oriental, but call it Peasant Caviar when you serve it — even confirmed eggplant haters will go wild about it, if you neglect to tell them what it is. You can serve it with squares of pumpernickel or Melba toast as an appetizer or put it on a bed of lettuce for a salad.

1 eggplant (about 1 pound)
2 tablespoons Garlic Oil (see page 54)
2 tablespoons Rosemary-Tarragon Vinegar (see above)
¼ cup minced onion
Salt and pepper to taste

Place the eggplant in a small pan and bake at 325°F. for 2 hours, or until collapsed. When it's cool enough to handle, cut a slit in the skin and scoop out the meat. Combine with all the other ingredients. Chill.

Serves 4 as a salad or 8 as an appetizer.

HOMEMADE CHICKEN STOCK

Chicken stock or broth is a versatile ingredient that can enrich soups and sauces or substitute for oil when you're sautéing vegetables. To make 4 quarts of rich chicken stock takes less than an hour of your time, although the cooking time is longer. The stock can be kept in the refrigerator for several weeks or frozen in small containers and kept for several months.

This broth is a tasty soup by itself. Add noodles for chicken noodle soup or puréed vegetables and herbs to make a hot or cold vegetable soup.

1 chicken carcass, 5 to 6 chicken pieces, or 1 whole chicken

4 quarts cold water
1 large sprig fresh rosemary (or 1 teaspoon dried)
1 large sprig fresh parsley (don't use dried)
1 large sprig fresh thyme (or 1 teaspoon dried)
1 medium-sized onion, peeled and cut in half
1 medium-sized carrot, peeled and cut into chunks (about
     ½ cup)
1 bay leaf
6 peppercorns
     Leafy tops of 3 celery ribs, cut up

Rinse the carcass, bones, or chicken pieces in cold water and place in a large kettle or stockpot. Add the water. Add the remaining ingredients and slowly bring to a boil. Turn down to a simmer and partially cover. Simmer for 2 hours.

If you are using chicken pieces, simmer for 15 minutes and remove the chicken from the kettle. When cool enough to handle, remove the meat from the bones and store it in the refrigerator for later use. Return the bones to the kettle and continue to simmer for 2 hours.

Strain the broth into a large bowl. Cool to room temperature, then refrigerate. A layer of fat will rise to the top and should be removed before reheating the broth. The stock can also be frozen.

Makes 4 quarts.

Quick and Easy Cream of Broccoli Soup

2¼ cups chicken stock
4 tablespoons butter
4 tablespoons flour
2 large stalks fresh broccoli, or 1 package frozen chopped
     broccoli
½ cup chopped onion
¾ teaspoon marjoram
¼ teaspoon oregano
     Dash white pepper
¼ cup heavy cream, buttermilk, or yogurt

Gently heat 2 cups of the stock in a small saucepan. Melt the butter in a medium saucepan. Add the flour to the butter and cook for about 2 minutes, stirring, until the roux is foamy and no longer smells of flour. It should not brown. Add the hot stock and cook over medium heat until the sauce begins to boil. Stir often. When it begins to boil, it is as thick as it will get. Turn off the heat.

While the stock is thickening, wash fresh broccoli and remove the leaves and the woody bottom of the stalk. Cut the broccoli into 1-inch pieces and place in a steamer basket with the onion. Steam for 10 minutes, or until soft. Cook frozen broccoli with the onion according to the package directions. Purée the broccoli and onion in a blender or food processor with the remaining ¼ cup of chicken stock.

Add the broccoli and onion to the thickened stock. Add the remaining ingredients and heat through. Do not boil. Serve hot.

Serves 4.

Cheddar Cheese Soup

This highly flavored soup takes almost an hour to make, but it is worth the effort if you are a cheese lover. Vermont sharp cheddar is best.

2	slices bacon
1	cup finely minced onion
1	cup finely minced celery
1	cup finely minced carrots
1	cup finely minced green pepper
6	cups Homemade Chicken Stock (see page 56)
6	tablespoons butter and 6 tablespoons oil or chicken fat
12	tablespoons flour
1	cup imported beer
4	cups grated cheddar cheese
½	teaspoon white pepper
2	tablespoons finely chopped fresh parsley
4	teaspoons finely chopped fresh dill
	Dash cayenne, or to taste

Chop the bacon into small pieces, about ¼ inch square. Place in a heavy-bottomed soup kettle or Dutch oven and cook until it is lightly browned. Add the minced vegetables and sauté in the bacon grease, stirring often, for 5 minutes. Add ½ cup of the chicken stock. Cover and simmer 10 to 15 minutes, until the vegetables are soft. Check to make sure they don't brown. Stir several times.

Add the butter and oil and stir until the butter melts. Add the flour and cook until the flour is absorbed into the butter, about 1 to 2 minutes. Stir constantly.

Heat the remaining 5½ cups chicken stock and the beer in a separate pot until warm. Then add the hot stock to the roux and stir as it thickens. When the soup begins to bubble gently, add the remaining ingredients. The cheese should be stirred in ½ cup at a time.

Serve this soup hot with a crusty bread and a salad of butter lettuce, orange slices, avocado slices, and purple onions with an oil and vinegar dressing.

Serves 8

Chilled Zucchini Soup

2 medium-sized zucchini, cut into 2-inch pieces (about 3 cups)
½ cup coarsely chopped onion
1 sprig fresh thyme (or 1 teaspoon dried)
1 sprig fresh parsley
1 bay leaf
3 cups Homemade Chicken Stock (see page 56)
1 tablespoon lemon juice
¼ teaspoon white pepper
1 cup plain yogurt

Place the zucchini, onion, thyme, parsley, and bay leaf in a medium-sized saucepan with 1 cup of the chicken stock. Bring to a boil, then simmer until the zucchini is tender, about 10 minutes. Remove the bay leaf and parsley and purée the mixture in a blender or food processor until it is of uniform consistency. Your kitchen will be filled with the aroma of thyme.

Strain the purée by pressing it through a strainer with the back of a spoon. Add the remaining chicken stock and the rest of the ingredients. Stir to blend. Chill for at least 1 hour.

Serve this refreshing soup with cold chicken and a light salad.

Serves 4.

Main Courses

Rosemary Chicken

2 whole chicken breasts, split into 4 pieces
2 tablespoons butter
1½ teaspoons dried rosemary
½ cup dry white wine
¼ cup slivered almonds
     Freshly grated pepper to taste

Preheat the oven to 325°F.

Wash the chicken breasts and pat them dry. Place them in an ovenproof shallow dish so the pieces are touching but not crowded. Dot the chicken with the butter. Sprinkle with the rosemary.

Bake for 45 minutes. Pour the wine over the chicken, sprinkle the almonds on top, and grate some pepper over everything. Raise the oven temperature to 350° F. and bake for another 15 minutes. Serve immediately.

This is a very simple and elegant dish.

Serves 4.

TABOULI

A summertime favorite, when herbs and tomatoes are fresh, this hearty main-course salad is a meal in itself. Bulgur wheat is available in most health-food stores.

If you use canned garbanzo beans, be sure to drain and rinse them first. If you use dried beans, they must be soaked overnight before cooking. Cook for about 1 hour to get them to the proper consistency. About ¼ cup of dried beans will equal 1 cup cooked.

1½   cups bulgur wheat
3   cups water
4   tablespoons olive oil
1   cup cooked garbanzo beans (chickpeas)
3   tomatoes, chopped and seeded
2   garlic cloves, minced
2   tablespoons chopped chives
1   tablespoon chopped fresh mint
¼   cup fresh lemon juice
¼   cup chopped fresh parsley

Place the bulgur and water in a saucepan and bring to a boil. Turn off the heat and let stand for 1 hour, until the bulgur has absorbed all the water.

Place the grain in a large bowl, toss with the olive oil, and chill for at least an hour.

Add the remaining ingredients and mix gently.

Serve on lettuce leaves or in pita bread pockets.

Serves 8.

BAKED CLAMS OREGANATA

These baked clams make a splendid main course. For an appetizer, just serve them in smaller ramekins.

½ cup minced onion
½ cup minced celery
3 tablespoons Garlic Oil (see page 54)
2 cups shucked clams, chopped, complete with their juices (or two 6½-ounce cans minced clams, juice and all)
½ cup freshly grated Parmesan cheese
2 slices homemade or fresh bakery bread, crumbled
1 teaspoon dried oregano
2 tablespoons Basil Vinegar (see page 55)
2 slices bacon, cut in half (optional)
Lemon wedges for serving

Cook the onion and celery in the Garlic Oil for a few minutes until limp. Add the clams. Stir over medium heat for 2 to 3 minutes, then add all the other ingredients except the bacon and the lemon wedges, stirring gently to mix. Put into 4 large scallop shells (which can be bought in most kitchenware stores) or ramekins. Top each with a half-slice of bacon, if desired. Bake at 425°F. for 10 minutes, or until lightly browned. Serve with lemon wedges.

Serves 4 as a main course.

CHICKEN BRAISED WITH BASIL VINEGAR

Fabulous dishes of this sort turn up in the cooking of both France and Italy. The flavor of the herb vinegar permeates the chicken and creates a small amount of simple but succulent sauce.

1 3-pound chicken, cut up or quartered
Salt and freshly ground black pepper to taste
4 tablespoons Garlic Oil (see page 54)
¼ cup Basil Vinegar (see page 55)

Rub the chicken with a little salt and pepper. Heat the Garlic Oil in a large frying pan over medium heat, then brown the chicken all over in this.

Remove the chicken pieces to a shallow baking dish, pour on the vinegar, and bake, uncovered, at 350°F. for 35 to 40 minutes, basting 3 or 4 times.

Serves 4.

HERB BATTER BREAD

This bread is made from a batter rather than a dough. Batter is stickier than dough and, therefore, requires very little kneading.

Instant minced onion works best in this recipe — the flavor is stronger than that of fresh onions and holds up better during baking.

1	tablespoon yeast
¼	cup warm water
1	cup low-fat cottage cheese
2	tablespoons sugar
2	tablespoons instant minced onion
2	tablespoons dill seed
1	tablespoon minced fresh dill weed
½	teaspoon dried oregano
¼	teaspoon baking soda
1	egg, unbeaten
1	tablespoon butter or margarine, softened
2¼	to 2½ cups all-purpose flour

Sprinkle the yeast over the warm water in a large bowl. While the yeast is dissolving, heat the cottage cheese to lukewarm in a medium-sized saucepan. Stir constantly. Add all of the remaining ingredients, except the flour, to the warm cottage cheese. Stir until the ingredients are well blended. Add the cheese mixture to the yeast and stir well.

Add the flour ½ cup at a time, beating with a wooden spoon after each addition. Roll the dough onto a lightly floured counter and knead it 10 times, until the dough is smooth and the flour absorbed.

Return the dough to the bowl and cover it with a damp towel. Place the bowl in a warm spot and let the dough rise until it has doubled in size (approximately 1 hour). Punch down the dough and shape it into a ball. Place it in a 1½-quart, 8-inch round casserole dish and let it rise for 30 to 40 minutes.

Preheat the oven to 350°F.

Bake for 40 to 50 minutes, or until the bread has browned on top and sounds hollow when tapped. Let the bread rest in the casserole dish for about 5 minutes. If you can wait, let the bread cool before slicing it; hot bread tends to fall apart during slicing.

This flavorful bread goes well with mild cheeses and cold cuts. It is also a good accompaniment to hearty soups or stews on chilly nights.

Makes 1 round loaf.

ZESTY RYE BREAD

2	tablespoons yeast
1½	cups warm water
¼	cup molasses
1	tablespoon sugar
¼	cup orange juice
4	teaspoons fennel seed
4	teaspoons anise seed
½	teaspoon cardamom seeds
2	tablespoons unsalted butter or margarine, softened
2¼	cups rye flour
2	cups unbleached all-purpose white flour

Sprinkle the yeast over the warm water in a large bowl. In a small bowl mix the remaining ingredients, except the flours. When the yeast is dissolved, add the molasses mixture to the yeast and stir well.

Add the rye flour ½ cup at a time, beating with a wooden spoon after each addition. Then add the all-purpose flour in the same manner. Roll the dough onto a lightly floured counter and knead for about 10 minutes, until the flour is absorbed and the dough is smooth, but not sticky.

Return the dough to the bowl and cover it with a damp towel. Let the dough rise in a warm place until it doubles in size (1 to 1½ hours). Punch down the dough and knead it several times to bring it back to its original size. Divide the dough in half and shape each half into a smooth oval. Place the loaves on a greased cookie sheet and let them rise for 1 hour.

Preheat the oven to 375°F.

Before baking, make three diagonal slashes across the top of each loaf. Bake for 30 minutes. Cool on racks.

This tasty bread blends beautifully with cheeses and sliced meats. It is delicious toasted and eaten with marmalade. A chilled soup, a crisp salad, and a slice of zesty rye bread make a memorable summer lunch.

Makes 2 oval loaves.

Oregano Cheddar Bread

1	package active dry yeast
5¼	cups all-purpose flour
2½	cups shredded sharp cheddar cheese
1¾	cups milk
3	tablespoons salad oil
2	tablespoons sugar
2	tablespoons dried oregano (or 4 tablespoons fresh, minced)
1	teaspoon salt

Stir together the yeast and 2 cups of the flour in a large mixing bowl. Heat together the remaining ingredients (except the rest of the flour) until lukewarm. Add to the flour-yeast mixture. Beat on low speed in a mixer for 30 seconds, scraping the bowl constantly. Then beat at high speed for 3 minutes. Stir in as much of the remaining flour as you can mix in with a spoon.

On a lightly floured surface, knead in enough of the remaining flour to make a stiff dough. Knead for another 8 to 9 minutes, until the dough is elastic and smooth. Shape into a ball and place in a lightly greased bowl, turning once to grease all sides of the dough's surface. Cover and let rise in a warm place until the dough is double in bulk (about 75 minutes).

Punch down the dough and divide it in half. Cover and let it sit for 10 minutes. Shape into 2 loaves and place in buttered 8" x 4" loaf pans. Cover the loaves and let them rise until nearly double in bulk, about 45 minutes.

Bake in a preheated 350° F. oven for 40 to 45 minutes. Cover with foil for last few minutes of baking to prevent overbrowning. Cool on a wire rack.

Makes 2 loaves.

Chapter 8

Crafts and Gift Ideas

One of the greatest pleasures derived from herbs comes from sharing them. The sweet scents of herbs can be captured for use in potpourris, bath oils, fragrant wreaths, or any number of attractive, aromatic crafts for gift giving or your own use. They'll fill the house with a breath of sweet, fresh air in any season. These projects are easy to make and offer plenty of room for creativity.

Potpourris

A potpourri is a blend of spicy flowers, a medley of pleasing scents. There are dozens of delightful, fragrant blends you can make from the herbs and flowers you grow yourself, with the addition of oils, spices, and fixatives. Mixing potpourri is to an herb lover what cooking is to a gourmet. You will soon find yourself making up your own recipes to utilize your favorite scents and plants.

Essential fragrant oils are expensive, but their essence lasts long after the herbs and flowers have lost their original scents. The fixative absorbs and "captures" the essence of the oil and preserves its aroma for many years.

Ground, chopped, or "pinhead" orris root is a favorite fixative (more so than in its powdered form) because it magically makes any plant or floral material smell like whatever oil you mix it with. This makes it possible to create a lovely "remembrance" potpourri for someone from a varied collection of dried flowers from a wedding or other special occasion. Just choose the oil most suited to the ingredients, and the orris root will do the rest! Other fixatives available include calamus root and gum benzoin, but they tend not to be as effective as orris root.

Basic Recipe for Potpourri

To 1 quart of crisp-dry flowers and herbs add 3 tablespoons of fixative, to which 1 teaspoon of essential oil has *first* been added, blended, covered, and stored for a few days, and shaken occasionally. (By allowing the orris root to absorb the moisture of the oil, your herbs and flowers will stay dried themselves.)

65

Add 2 or 3 tablespoons of spices to the herbs and flowers. Mix everything together well and store in a covered nonmetallic container for 4 to 6 weeks, stirring or mixing occasionally.

The potpourri is then mixed well or "set" to put in jars for gifts, or crushed to a fine consistency, if preferred, for sachets. (If you leave the ingredients whole, the recipients can more easily identify them.)

Basic Rose Potpourri

If you are a beginner, divide this basic recipe into parts and try the variations separately. You will soon find which scents are the most appealing to you.

Blend 1 teaspoon rose oil with 3 tablespoons ground orris root and allow to "set" for a few days, covered (empty spice jars are good to use for this). Then add the orris-root mixture to 1 quart crisp-dry rose petals.

Rose Geranium

Variations

- For a *spicy* scent: add 2 tablespoons each ground cloves and cinnamon.
- For a very *sweet* scent: add 2 cups lavender blossoms and ¼ cup ground tonka or vanilla beans.
- For a *fruity* scent: add 1 cup each dried citrus peel, rose- and lemon-scented geranium leaves, and lemon balm or lemon verbena.

Or mix all of the ingredients named in the variations together (plus extra rose petals, oil, and orris root). You will soon find yourself adding "a bit of this" and "a touch of that" as you discover your favorite combinations.

Basic Lavender Potpourri

Add 1 quart lavender blossoms to 3 tablespoons orris root that has been pre-mixed with 10 drops lavender oil.

Variations

- Add a cup or two of dried lilac, larkspur, cornflower, or any floral blossoms for additional color, or rose petals for fragrance, plus double the amount of orris root and oil.

- A tablespoon of ground cloves will add a spicy touch.
- ½ cup of ground vanilla beans will sweeten the blend.
- A cup of bergamot leaves and/or mint will add freshness.

Lavender, rose, cloves, and vanilla (or tonka) beans are all "naturals" together, so for a *super* Lavender-Rose Potpourri, combine the two basic rose and lavender recipes and add 2 tablespoons cloves and 1 cup ground tonka beans.

BLENDERS FOR POTPOURRI

Once you decide on a basic fragrance for a potpourri (floral, woodsy, citrus, or what you will), this primary scent will be the star of the show and determine everything else to be added to

POTPOURRI BLENDING

BASIC SCENT	PRIMARY FLOWERS & HERBS (6 cups)	BLENDERS (3 cups)	FIXATIVES (½ cup of roots or gums; 1 cup woods; 3 cups leaves)	OILS (1 tsp.)
Fruity	Lemon verbena, lemon balm, yellow/orange flower petals	Citrus-scented geraniums, lemongrass, orange mint, citrus peel	Calamus root, clary sage, oakmoss	Sweet orange, lemon, or bitter almond
Floral	Rose petals, lavender, rose-scented geraniums	Tonka beans, patchouli, cinnamon, cloves	Santal chips, calamus root, gum benzoin, frankincense	Ambergris, civet, rose
Woodsy	Any sweetly scented petals	Patchouli, cassia, oakmoss, mace	Sandalwood, vetiver root	Benzoin, frankincense

the blend. Blenders, or modifiers, are the "supporting cast" — the harmonious herbs, spices, flowers, seeds, woods, or citrus peel that are used in smaller quantities. These complement the basic scent, adding zest, variety, balance, color, or texture. The fixatives and essential oils are the "magic," the cohesive elements that tie everything together .

If you're creating your own potpourri, a general basic recipe might call for 6 cups of flowers and herbs of the basic scent, a total of 3 cups of blenders, and ½ cup of fixative(s), in which you have first mixed 1 teaspoon of essential oil(s).

You might want to experiment with some of the following combinations, adjusting the amounts to suit your senses. Some fixatives are also blenders, and vice versa, depending on the holding power, the strength, and the amounts used.

SOME POPULAR POTPOURRI MIXES

BASIC PINE POTPOURRI

Especially appreciated at Christmastime!

2 quarts ground pine needles
1 cup orris root, combined with 1 tablespoon pine oil

FRUITY PINE POTPOURRI

2 cups each: pine needles
spearmint leaves
lemon verbena (or lemon balm)
As much lemon and orange peel as desired
¾ cup orris root, blended with
2 teaspoons pine oil and
1 teaspoon lemon oil

CITRUSCENT

Offer this potpourri as "stored summer sunshine" to combat winter blues and remind the recipients of next spring's promise. Add extra flowers for more vivid color.

4 cups lemon verbena leaves
2 cups lemon balm leaves
2 cups orange mint leaves
2 cups lemon-, lime-, and/or orange-scented geranium leaves
1 cup pineapple or apple mint leaves
4 cups ground citrus peel
4 cups marigold or calendula petals (or other yellow and orange flowers like lilies, daffodils, or forsythia)
2 cups orris root, mixed with 1 tablespoon sweet orange oil and 1 tablespoon sweet lemon oil

The perfect solution to the winter doldrums or a hard day: curl up with a favorite book in a fragrant herbal bath.

HERBAL SOAP BALLS

Pour ¼ cup boiling water over 1 tablespoon dried, pulverized herbs (chamomile or lavender flowers, leaves of peppermint, rosemary, sage, or thyme, or a combination of the last five ingredients). Add 5 or 6 drops of a related essential oil, if desired, for a stronger scent. Steep for 15 minutes. Reheat until

---

MINTCENSE

The colonists claimed that mint potpourri "cleared the head," and they placed it in covered china or apothecary jars as desk accessories. In the same tradition, this blend is an excellent room freshener when shaken and opened. Red bergamot flowers make a Christmasy addition.

2 cups each peppermint, orange mint, and spearmint leaves, and lavender blossoms
1 cup each thyme and rosemary leaves
½ cup orris root, blended with 1 tablespoon oil of lavender or pennyroyal

BERGAMOT

---

bubbly and pour over 2 cups shredded Ivory soap (1 "personal-size" bar). Mix well with your hands and let stand for 15 minutes. Mix again and divide into 3 or 6 parts, rolling each into a ball. Place on plastic wrap and let dry for 3 days.

BATH BAGS

Cut muslin or cheesecloth bags large enough to hold ½ to 1 cup of herbs. Secure tightly with a ribbon or string long enough to hang from the faucet, so that the hot tap water will "steep" the oils and fragrances of the herbs, adding their benefits to your bath. An equal amount of fine oatmeal added to the herbs will act as a water softener and skin smoother. Powdered milk may be included to simulate the skin-softening effects of a milk bath.

For softer skin, use chamomile, calendula, and elder flowers in a blend with oatmeal and powdered milk. Rubbing the wet bag over your skin will bring extra benefits! *For a stimulating bath,* use rosemary, lemon verbena, marjoram, fennel, and lemon peel (or substitute thyme or sage). *For a relaxing bath,* use chamomile, calendula, and lime flowers, rose geranium leaves, and a pinch of powdered valerian root or catnip leaves.

You can make an *infusion* by pouring 4 cups of boiling water over 4 tablespoons of herb leaves and flowers. Steep for ½ hour, strain, and add to the bath water.

Make a *decoction* by boiling 1 cup of herb seeds, barks, or roots in 4 cups of water for 20 minutes. Strain and add to bath water. *For weary bones and aching muscles,* make a decoction of comfrey, sage, nettle, horsetail, and pine needles.

CALENDULA OR POT MARIGOLD

DISPERSABLE BATH OIL

This oil will permeate the water. Combine 4 parts Turkey Red Oil (available from most pharmacists) and 1 part fragrant essential oil of your choice, such as lavender, jasmine, or sandalwood. (Add a sprig of fresh herb if desired.)

FLOATING BATH OIL

One teaspoon of almond oil will float on the water and coat your body as you leave the tub (or you can rub it on your body before the bath). Scent the oil with an essential fragrance of your choice.

HERBAL FOOTBATH

Add a handful of any or all of the following, tied in a cloth bag, to your footbath to soothe tired feet: fresh or dried comfrey, lavender, pennyroyal, rosemary, and sage.

LAVENDER BATH

Use equal amounts of lavender blossoms, comfrey leaves, and Epsom salts, plus several drops of lavender oil. Blend well and store in a pretty container. Use a handful per bath to restore aching limbs.

Lavender Beauty Bath

Mix thoroughly 1 cup baking soda, 1 quart Epsom salts, and 1 dram lavender oil. Place in a large bowl with a scoop. Add a scoopful to your hot bath and enjoy a fragrant, soothing soak. The mixture can be tied in muslin or cotton squares, too.

Sachets to Share

Sachets can be made by simply pinking the edges of 6" x 6" squares of fabrics, sheer enough to permit the fragrance to emanate through, such as organdy, muslin, or cotton polyester.

How to Make Sachets

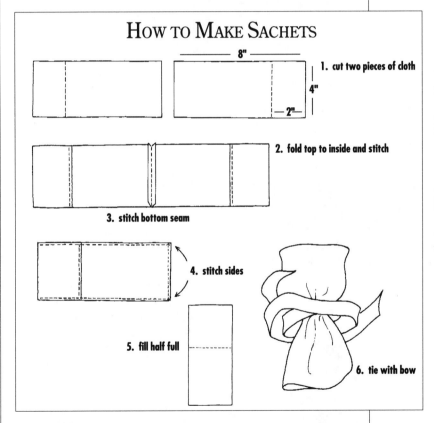

8"

1. cut two pieces of cloth

4"

2"

2. fold top to inside and stitch

3. stitch bottom seam

4. stitch sides

5. fill half full

6. tie with bow

Once you've prepared your potpourri, place 2 or 3 tablespoons in the center of each square, pull the corners up, and tie them securely in the center with heavy thread. A pretty velvet or satin matching ribbon is the finishing touch. Or, you can machine-stitch heart, oblong, or circular shapes to create your own special bags.

Basic Sweet Bag Potpourri

These are wonderful for hanging in a closet, bureau drawer, car, suitcase, or purse.

2	quarts rose-scented geranium leaves
1	quart lemon verbena or lemon balm
1	pint lavender flowers
1	pint pineapple sage or pineapple mint leaves
2	cups ground citrus peel
1	cup ground tonka beans
1 or 2	cups basil, chamomile, marjoram, or tarragon (optional)

Variations

1	teaspoon rose geranium oil added to ½ cup orris root and/or
1	teaspoon orange oil added to ½ cup orris root

Both of these variations will add longer life and more vivid fragrance, if desired.

Lavender Tree

This tree looks particularly stunning on a long dining room table or a grand piano. And it is a pleasure to create in the early fall, to have ready and waiting for the often-hectic holiday season.

Make a large wire mesh cone (14 inches tall) from ½-inch hardware cloth. Using wire scissors and pliers, intertwist and bend back the cut ends to fasten the cone. Anchor the cone to a circular base — masking tape and an old metal pizza pan work well.

You will need several buckets of Silver King Artemisia for a tree 32 inches tall and 36 inches wide.

Starting at the bottom, place the longest branches through the center of the cone. Working upward, use the next-to-largest branches on the next tier, and so on, leaving the shortest and prettiest blossoms for the top. Reserve 3 to 5

Start at bottom, placing longest branches through center of cone.

Finished lavender tree with tussie-mussies.

medium-length branches to add height to the top.

Next, place bunches of ribboned or netted dried flowering herbs in among the branches. They will be kept in place by the curlicues of artemisia. Try using bunches of lavender, purple basil, oregano, pennyroyal, peppermint, and orange mint — all shades of purple or lavender, with matching ribbon and netting.

Place favors to be offered as gifts on the tree and in sterling silver bowls on the table around it — lavender sachets and small tussie-mussies made with baby's breath and the herbs mentioned. The tree fits nicely on a card table, which you can camouflage with a gray lace tablecloth, topped by three layers of purple netting. Revive the tree every season with lavender oil on the sachets, and store it in a dark room.

Southernwood Wreaths

It is best to use *fresh* southernwood, as it is less fragile and more pliable than dried, allowing you gently to bend or break the woody branches to flow in the curved shapes you want.

Tie together several bunches of 10 to 14-inch branches with florist wire or twist-ties. Then anchor them to a wire or woody wreath frame. Overlap the bunches of branches, making them all go in the same direction.

Keep the wreaths in a dry, dark, airy spot for a week or so. Air conditioning, a fan, or a dehumidifier will facilitate the drying process. When crisp and dry, the wreaths will hold their shape, but they should be transferred to plates or baskets as permanent bases, because they will be fragile.

Decorate as you wish. A suggestion: decorate with bunches of dried silvermound artemisia and red bergamot flowers. The southernwood dries to an olive green, quite a unique hue.

Potpourri Southernwood Wreath

Set two lemon- or tangerine-scented southernwood wreaths, with the smaller one on top, on a mat or plate base, then place a bowl of potpourri in the center. Decorate with dried roses, bunches of lavender blossoms, sprigs of lemon verbena, orange mint, and lamb's ears. Enclose a note telling the recipient that the entire wreath can be crumbled up and added to the potpourri when the wreath is "spent." If stored carefully, it could last for several seasons, so you might wish to enclose a small vial of rose oil and some orris root for restoring the fragrance.

Basic Steps in Wreath Making

1. Use a straw wreath form (illustrated) or a wire or wood wreath frame.

2. Tie together bunches of herbs with floral wire and, starting from the inside of the wreath, insert the bunches with stems all going in the same direction.

3. Still going in one direction, insert larger plants around outside of wreath.

4. Keep wreath in a dry, dark, airy spot to dry for a week or so.

5. Decorate and hang!

A LIVING WREATH

A live wreath started in mid-October will be lush for the holidays. Purchase a 12-inch planting frame from the florist. Fill with well-soaked sphagnum moss and place in a shallow bowl. Insert cuttings of herbs, using rooting hormones (see page 36).

Try using myrtle on the inside and outside, with culinary or tea herbs in groups of three on the top: scented geraniums, thyme, sage, and rosemary.

Keep the wreath under a grow-light, water it with a weak solution of fertilizer, mist it regularly, and trim the tops as needed, to keep the plants compact.

A LIVING WREATH

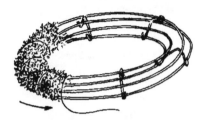

Fill frame with well-soaked sphagnum moss, securing with green floral wire.

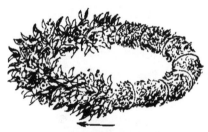

Insert cuttings, with stems all going in one direction as shown.

Finished wreath ready to be placed under indoor lights and watered with weak solution of fertilizer until holiday time.

Sources for Herb Seeds

Mail-Order Sources for Plants, Seedlings, and Seeds

Alberta Nurseries Ltd.
P.O. Box 20
Bowden, Alberta
Canada T0M 0K0
(Catalog $2.00)

Butterflies 'n Blossoms
Route 1, P.O. Box 236
Fayetteville, TN 37334
(Catalog $1.50)

Caprilands Herb Farm
Silver Street
Coventry, CT 06238
(Catalog $.50)

Carroll Gardens
P.O. Box 310
Westminster, MD 21157
(Catalog $2.00)

Cedarbrook Herb Farm
986 Sequim Avenue South
Sequim, WA 98382

Clement Herb Farm
Route 6, P.O. Box 390
Rogers, AR 72756
(Catalog $.50)

Country Manor
Route 211, Box 520
Sperryville, VA 22740
(Catalog $2.00)

Flower Valley Herb Parfumerie
Route 2, Box 22
Dixon, IA 52745
(Catalog $1.00)

Gatehouse Herbs
98 Van Buren Street
Dolgeville, NY 13329
(SASE)

Good Scents
P.O. Box 854
Rialto, CA 92376
(Catalog $.50)

Greenfield Herb Garden
Depot & Harrison, Box 437
Shipshewana, IN 45454

Griffin's
5109 Vickrey Chapel Road
Greensboro, NC 27407
(Catalog $2.00)

Heartscents
P.O. Box 1674
Hilo, HI 96721
(Catalog $1.00)

The Herb Cottage
Washington Cathedral
Mount Saint Alban
Washington, DC 20016
(Catalog $.25)

The Herb Connection
2627 John Petree Road
Powder Spring, GA 30073
(Catalog $2.00)

Herb Gathering/Gourmet Seeds
5742 Kenwood, Box 236
Kansas City, MO 64110
(Catalog $.50)

Herbitage Farm
Rd 2
Richmond, NH 03470
(Catalog $1.00)

Herbs 'n' Spice
P.O. Box 3358
Sparks, NV 89432
(Catalog $1.00)

Logee's Greenhouses
55 North Street
Danielson, CT 06239
(Catalog $3.00)

Meadowbrook Herb Garden
Rte. 138
Wyoming, RI 02898
(Catalog $1.00)

Merry Gardens
P.O. Box 595
Camden, ME 04842
(Catalog $2.00)

New York Botanical Gardens
Southern Blvd.
at 200th Street
Bronx, NY 10458
(SASE)

Old Sturbridge Village
Sturbridge, MA 01566

Plants of the Southwest
1570 Pacheco Street
Santa Fe, NM 87501
(Catalog $1.00)

Otto Richter & Sons Ltd.
P.O. Box 26
Goodwood, Ontario
Canada L0C 1A0
(Catalog $2.00)

St. John's Herb Garden
The Perfume Garden
7711 Hillmeade Road
Bowie, MD 20715

Taylor's Herb Garden, Inc.
1535 Lone Oak Road
Vista, CA 92083
(Catalog $1.00)

Well-Sweep Herb Farm
317 Mt. Bethel Road
Port Murray, NJ 07865
(Catalog $1.00)

POTPOURRI AND CRAFT SUPPLIES

Bay Laurel Farm
Glory Condon
West Garzas Road
Carmel Valley, CA 93924
(Wreaths; Catalog $1.00)

Caprilands Herb Farm
Silver Street
Coventry, CT 06238
(Catalog $.50)

Caswell-Massey Co. Ltd.
21 Fulton Street
South St. Seaport
New York, NY 10038
(Catalog $1.00)

Gingham 'n Spice, Ltd.
P.O. Box 88
Gardenville, PA 18926
(Oils; Catalog $1.50)

Good Scents
P.O. Box 854
Rialto, CA 92376
(Potpourri supplies;
Catalog $.50)

Meadow Everlastings
149 Shabbona Road
Malta, IL 60150
(Dried flowers; Catalog $1.00)

Rosemary Lane
P.O. Box 493
Rockwall, TX 75087
(Wreaths; Catalog $1.50)

St. John's Herb Garden
The Perfume Garden
7711 Hillmeade Road
Bowie, MD 20715
(Oils)

INDEX